How to Restore a Castle: Part Two

A Somewhat Definitive & Definitely Partial
Restoration Manual for Owners of Ruined
Historic Buildings, Particularly Those on the
West Coast of Scotland

Charles Dixon-Spain

In Loving Memory
M. O. H.

CONTENTS

The most difficult thing is the decision to act, the rest is mere tenacity.

Amelia Earhart

Introduction to Part the Second of How to Restore a Castle

In the first part of *How to Restore a Castle*, I told the tale of how Sadie and I acquired Dunans Castle in Argyll having discovered the ruin in May 2002. Through a series of Admonitions, set out as a How-to manual, I narrated the tale of our progress in the face of disappointment, misdirection, and intimidation. Sadie and I uncovered the recent history of the building which had been ill-served by its previous owners and, as the reader will have found, we stood firm in the face of midges, wrecked services, and prognostication by signage, while drawing comfort from family, friends and the people we met in the local community.

In part two I continue with my admonitions, detailing our efforts to remain warm during our first winter, the intelligence we garnered from phone calls, hitchhikers and vandalism, and the progress we made towards making a life, at the head of the glen, beside our dear old tumble-down pile of stones – also known as a castle.

Admonition the Thirtieth: A Note on Offal, Sausages, Loaves and Puddings

Perhaps this seems an odd place to begin *How To Restore A Castle: Part Two* – with a note on various types of offally foods – but it is a critical moment in our adventure, one which depends on the use of metaphor and pseudonym to properly and frankly tell the tale.

In "Admonition the Third: Notes Can Be of Utmost Importance", I point out that I will be describing events and characters in service to the truth as I see it, which may be different from an objectively verifiable narrative. Moreover, I undertake not to identify all participants in the narrative directly. And having thought about this extensively since writing that, I think there is one class of characters who require their own particular nomenclature.

One such character we have had reference to, a certain Mr. Haslet – he is named after that delicious, but surprisingly-not-ubiquitous, sausage-based loaf traditionally created in Lincolnshire. And Haslet embodies the convention I am introducing in that like the offal and meat-based foodstuff referenced by his name, he is a mishmash of characters, a collation of facets, spiced with different identities, and baked in the warming shelf of the Raeburn that is my writerly imagination.

Haslet therefore refers not to one person, but to

several. That some of those ingredients might be considered unsavoury might not be entirely coincidental, nor that these foodstuffs are traditional, are often an acquired taste, are delicacies of an older generation, is also important. The same can be said for characters not yet introduced in *How to Restore a Castle*, for example Mr. Haggis and Mr. Lorne. The former is soon to make his entrance, albeit shrouded in mystery and misdirection, but the latter, a reference to a sausage loaf popular in the Full Scottish Breakfast, may yet take some time to materialise – I am not sure at the time of writing. There will be others of course, so watch for the offal referent, the meat-based component, the intestinal sheath or rendered ingredient to be sure that the person referred to is part of this *offal brethren*.

Admonition the Thirty-first:
A Knowledge of the Trades
is Essential

The mechanics of getting our household north, from the Goldhawk Road to Glendaruel involved the hire of a luton van over three successive weekends, the storage of our gear in Michael the Hotel's barn, an open-ended let of the hotel's self-catering cottage and a final cramped journey in aforementioned Luton with bassets and Sadie to arrive at dusk on a sunny, spring evening at the hotel with a sense that while everything was possible it was also now properly irrevocable.

The next day at Dunans, under a blue sky, in fresh spring air and with heavy dew underfoot, a flatbed delivered wood, gravel mix, cement, and fixings. I signed the line for the materials once they'd been unloaded and watched as the lorry wallowed away down the drive feeling that now the adventure had properly – *properly* – begun.

A fortnight later, another flatbed arrived, loaded with a stack of panels, some rolls of mineral felt, clouts, mastic and three men. And six hours after that, the red shed had been assembled on my new rickety founds, and I was left with some shiny keys watching as the lorry and its crew wallowed away down the drive. I am not sure what I was feeling then, except that we now had an awfully big space to fit out on a very slim set of founds.

And two days after that, Magic Mike arrived. He spent a couple of hours inspecting our recently erected and startlingly red wooden chalet. Then he spent a further hour examining the shed's under-storey and its supporting cast of mismatched joists in their varied dimensions.

Fig. 1 – The Red Shed

Consequently, my first job was, apparently, to "… get under that shed and start supporting all those feeble four-by-twos you…What's the word? …installed? …while I work out what our options actually are."

This was the job on which I was to properly learn what had been implicit in the three renovation projects Sadie and I had completed thus far – meaning that, while I'd built small stud walls, created doorways, installed lintels, built decks, laid oak floors, and formed steps, none of it had been from scratch, and none had really interacted with electrics and plumbing. Very kindly, Mike led me step-by-step through the process, such that by the time we'd finished I was on my way to becoming a fair joiner. The plumbing not so much. The electrics not at all.

It took six weeks, start to finish, for the initial fit-out of our glorified garden shed: we had bedrooms at either end, a bathroom to the back, a galley kitchen in the main room with space for living and dining. Our hot-water cylinder sat above and to the left of our stove in the living area, and the stove was linked to five radiators which distributed heat around the space – or that was the idea. In the north end of the shed we had a spare bedroom and office under a conventional ceiling, with header-tank and a little storage above, and in the south end, where master bed and bathroom divided the space, the ceiling followed roof line. It was fine.

For a year or two.

We thought.

Admonition the Thirty-second: The Truth Will Out

Sadie returned to the fit-out of the red shed one afternoon having been to Dunoon to pick up our friend Kate – who was visiting for the weekend – full of the story of a hitchhiker who they'd given a lift to. The gentleman in question was swaying along in a westerly direction at the head of Loch Striven, a half bottle of something clasped in one hand and rucksack over his shoulder.

Sadie pulled over in response to the grubby, jutting thumb with the thought that wherever he was going, being that drunk would mean he'd more likely end up in the ditch rather than his destination, and that it was better he got to where he was going.

As the car slowed to a halt beside him, he turned in that slightly unfocussed way of someone several hours into his session and smiled at the driver and her passenger somewhat toothily. In short order he'd introduced himself as Wee Willie the Sweep[1] and informed them that he was walking to the Clachan in search of a "wee dram",[2] "some

---

[1] With apologies to native Scots speakers for my bowdlerization of a language which while adjacent to English, is, to my mind, more characterful, and, at times, more poetic. I've tried to capture an idea of it here, but it is only a pale imitation of the original.

[2] Small Alcoholic beverage

comp'ny" and "mebbe a bed for the night at wee Michael's", or failing that "… in a cruive[3] up in the hill by Modan's Well". When asked where he'd come from, he thought for a moment and replied, "Clachaig!" Well, that was where he'd spent the night, he said, in "tha' cozy bothy[4] with the timetable beside it." After some negotiation with door, seat and dogs, Willie was installed in the back seat, with bag and bottle in his lap and they roared off up the hill past Craigendive. With the car top down and the hounds on the back seat, the car might have been cozy, but it was still well-enough ventilated to disperse whatever fumes arose from the inebriated passenger.

As they wound their way towards the junction with the main road, Willie asked Sadie where she stayed, and when she said at Dunans, he rejoined, "Oh, are ye a Lady then?" Sadie replied she was not a Lady, well not of the type she thought he was referring to, and he agreed, saying "O no, no' that Lady then, she o' the bare foot and the sleekit[5] eye. She would'nae ha' stopped for the likes of me. Naw, she would'nae. But then," he ruminated, "I marked my card there. It were they tha' got me to clean their chimbleys and did'nae pay oot because it on'y made the smoking worse – sweeping them lums[6] I mean." He said, "… tha' building was always going tae burn down, 'less an' if the owners got those 'stacks lined, and the Fletchers and the folks efter never had the money." Though he did hear tell that the last lot, "… those that let it burn, did have a plan, the summer afore, no, wait, efter the fire. No, well, whit shall we say? So, it burned in the January, and the plan was made – afore the fire – for the summer of thet

---

[3] Rude Enclosure or Hovel

[4] Usually a stone hut in a remote place originally used by shepherds, but now more often used by walkers. In this case Willie has mistaken a bus shelter for a bothy.

[5] Glossy

[6] Chimneys

year, the year o' the fire. But efter the fire, and so," he sighed sadly, "it ne'er happened. Sech a pity to lose the house like tha' – great loss tae the glen – auld[7] Archie would ha' turned o'er in his mausie'leum. The poor old gaffer … See, I heard tha' they'd booked Scaffers to come o'er frae aff Bute and a gang contracted in frae[8] Glasgae to drop the liners. Never happened and wisnae tha' a shame? They should ha' got them in afore the winter and hang the 'kin expense."

When Sadie and Kate nodded uncertainly, he said, "A-ha! But then, I'd ha' ne'er got a lift from youse lassies[9] if they ha' done tha', ye ken?[10] eh?" and laughed uproariously.

---

[7] Old

[8] from

[9] girls

[10] You understand, don't you?

Admonition the Thirty-third: Sheds Should Always Be Surprising

That weekend, the weekend of Kate's visit and consequently the lift to Wee Willie the Sweep, we finally moved into the shed. Well, that was the aim. Kate had been invited to celebrate our new adventure and see us into our brand-spanking new residence.

As it happened, we weren't quite finished.

Not only had we had to sort out our water supply – *see* "Admonition the Twenty-eighth" – but we were short of an internal wall or two because my quantity surveying skills were not quite up to scratch at that point – as illustrated by my precipitous trip to the 'Goil rather than the 'Gilp some weeks before to remedy that perilous shortfall of *foundational* materials. That all said, Kate was up for camping, and Sadie was raring to go and give the stove and new kitchen a tryout.

I spent the evening with Mike at the bar in the Hotel ensuring we were sufficiently recharged for the labour of the following morning with flavourful beverages from Fyne Ales and filling sustenance prepared by Michael the Hotel.

We'd left Kate and Sadie with kindling, lumber off-cuts and plenty of alcohol to get them through the night.

And get through the night they did, until about 4 a.m.

when they were awoken by cracks and scratches and groans from directly underneath the shed. The noises were intermittent, random, and occasionally very loud. It was as if something or someone was kicking the joists. Or was butting the upstands. Or something.

With Kate awake too, they tried to work out what was causing the noise: they posited foxes, and then badgers, discounted owls or deer, decided cats, capercaillie and pheasants very unlikely, settled on sheep then discarded that idea along with cows given the constrained space. Rats were not an explanation given their absence in the glen. They finally alighted on revenants buried in the ground under the shed by some previously undiscovered sect of devil-worshipping Celtic Druidry disturbed by the proximity of living flesh and blood – with particular reference to brains. They chuckled and went back to sleep, still serenaded by the inexplicable, but infrequent noises.

The day dawned fresh and clear, with the sun slanting in through the back windows of the red shed. Sadie woke Kate with a cup of coffee, and they drank it on the freshly built front step, breathing in the pine-scented air, and watched dew, floating webs and multitudinous insect life drift across the view of the monumental Douglas Firs planted by Angus Fletcher. As they chatted about their tumultuous night and their discovery that their zombie-infestation had actually been the rank of five-litre plastic bottles left under the shed the day before, they became aware of a slow crunch of tyre over gravel. The sound became louder if no less furtive, until the nose of a grey estate emerged from behind the rank of *leylandii* along the drive.

Sadie stood immediately, shading her eyes, trying to see who it was who'd have the temerity to drive down at just past seven on a Sunday morning. She later reported that as soon as the windscreen slid into view the car stopped, dead – nose dipping at the sudden brake action.

"As if," she said, "the driver was shocked to see a

bloody great red shed had been erected in the grounds overnight. There was a pause – the kind of pause in which you could sense they were deciding whether it was to be fight or flight. Whoever it was chose flight. It felt like they'd been shocked to see the shed, and then, even more shocked to find there were people looking right back at them. The gears crunched and the car backed away. We could hear it all the way back to the corner – the car making that whine they do when they reverse too quickly. There was more crunching, squeaking, spilling of gravel, and then the roar of the engine as they went back over the bridge at high speed.

"By the time Kate and I got to look down the drive whoever it was was gone … It was all very odd."

"Salvagers?" I asked.

"Car was too smart, too new." said Kate, "Looked like a Saab or an Audi. Not your average builders' wagon by any means – well, not any builders I know."

"Then who was it, do we think?" I asked.

"No idea. A nosey-parker?" replied Sadie, "But on a Sunday. At Seven?"

Admonition the Thirty-fourth: If More Sheds Are Needed Then Do Not Resist

The well-bred shed is an artform. Obviously, there's the one you live in. That's the *essential* shed, insulated, heated, with services. Warm, liveable, albeit often late. But we have already described what became known as the Red Shed – there's even been an illustration!

There are, of course, other key sheds. First and foremost, in our shed hierarchy is the site office shed, for safety, and work, and admin, and meetings when it's raining. And cups of tea, and sandwiches and informal on-the-threshold discussions (*see* "Stalkers are not easily stalked"). This is the shed for the warming of hands, for the end of workday planning, and for planning and designing, and for retreating to when the midges get really, really bad. It's also the shed to develop business, to host workers for production and for customer service. Eventually this is the shed where tours finish, for the asking of questions, the discussion of progress and the identification of further plot locations. But to get there, this shed will require to be moved, from a location in front the red shed, uphill to a more retired, less visible locus, where veranda and covered area bring the outside in, and the project into focus.

But let's leave the thought of migratory sheds there shall we and move on to other important shedding typologies?

Next, there is the tool shed, for tools ... and also for kit. A tool shed can never be big enough, especially when you get to plant. Or you could build a plant shed (as distinct from a potting shed – which we will come to). No, a plant shed should have a concrete floor, a work bench and space for aforementioned plant, alongside twenty litre drums of assorted oils and fuels and lubricants. Tools can be part of this, but we found that with several sheds, we developed tool collections which migrated to the most appropriate storage. Obviously mechanical tools range in and around the plant shed. The tools for ground works have their own space.

Then there are the storage sheds, and the temporary storage sheds, and the semi-permanent storage tents, and then the tarp sheds or more simply, the tarps. These sheds can flower like mushrooms, almost overnight, and then in a matter of hours deliquesce when they are no longer required – or when we are hit by a particularly bad squall and they get distributed over the pasture, the drive or the rhodies. This inadvertent distribution is *not* migration – that is an entirely different *modus operandi.* Some storage sheds do persist however, especially those which shelter in the lee of a curtain wall, or under a gable, or in a bush.

Of these latter, the wardrobe shed was a particularly memorable example of the species. as it was attached to the red shed, and accessible from the same. This six-metre-by-six-metre space had to be painted the same bright ochre as our dwelling. Rather than engage in the complexity of an a-frame, I decided that this shed should enjoy the simplicity of a single sloped roof. The shed's floor was a deck, like the red shed, but instead of using chipboard I resorted to 12mm marine ply – which in turn meant that while the understory was properly specified, I still managed to produce an uneven floor where the progressively damp ply shifted and warped. The slope of the roof was at quite a rake, maybe twenty-five degrees, possibly more, and at its highest two hundred and forty centimetres above floor height. This meant the roof reached over three metres at its tallest extent. The back wall was a mere one-hundred-and-twenty centimetres high. Now bear in mind the sloped roof, the colour of the walls, and you should have, alongside the vision of the conventional(-ish) red shed, a ruddy great slice of red cheddar hovering a foot above the ground on its side. And cheese is the activating visual quality with which this spectacularly specified wardrobe should be considered. You see, despite the highly accurate joinery of yours truly, despite the legs the wedge was lifted by, despite mastic and sundry other sealing compounds, strategies and solutions, the red wedge seemed to act like a mouse magnet. Within weeks, if not days, of my shoes being stacked and racked in the darkest corner of our newly created clothing compendium, the scraggiest (or should I say cheesiest) of my trainers had been munched on, littered with droppings, and rendered unwearable.

Fortunately, the wedge shed (or "sheddar" as I privately christened it) was superseded when we moved our main bedroom to the other end of the red shed and created a walk-in wardrobe of the (now) spare room.

But to continue with more conventional sheds: the potting shed is for potting, and pottering, and pootering and procrastinating. This was the least and most important shed we *never* built. And we didn't build it partly because neither of us are plantspersons, and partly because the last potting shed stood at what would be the north end of the red shed, and that shed, though we never saw it, had a certain past, redolent of special brew, beanies, blue overalls, and roll-ups – *see* "Every Castle Should Have a Ghost" for more.

Finally, there's the woodshed – open-walled, stacked with split and unsplit logs. These sheds are particularly persistent, arising as wind fells overmature trees, or limbs, or roofs. And they move from site to site until, after a time, a decade-and-a-half say, they finally root themselves around the boneyard as windbreak, seasoning cover, and consolidated storage.

Admonition the Thirty-fifth: Not All Visitations will be Welcome

So, we moved into the red shed some six weeks after it had been delivered and erected. A couple of days later I took Mike to the ferry, after we had officially transferred our goods and chattels from the cottage at the hotel. Notwithstanding works we still needed doing, he'd been called back to Kildonan and a plumbing emergency at the Breadalbin – the many-storied, and most southerly, public house on the Isle of Arran. Besides, we wanted some time to consolidate ourselves in our new temporary accommodation, on our freshly acquired property. I returned from Portavadie in the mid-morning to find Sadie sitting on the front doorsteps, hands around a cup of coffee and a pensive expression on her face. As I walked up I asked, "Are you okay love?"

"Not sure." she replied. I sat down beside her and unpicked her hands from the lukewarm coffee cup, and held them, she smiled and said, "I've just had a visitation."

"Oh?"

"Some bloke …" she picked her coffee back.

"Oh?" my voice hardened. I could see she wasn't happy.

"Oh, don't worry he went. It was just that he stood there …" she nodded at the turning from drive to embrasure, "… and he stared."

"Stared?"

"Yes, completely unabashed. Well, I was at the window when I saw him, barefoot, coffee in hand." she raised the cup indicating that this was the coffee, "So, I put on my shoes. Quietly. Didn't want to get the dogs all excited. Then I opened the door and stepped out."

"And what happened?"

"Well, nothing. He just stared. As I say, completely unabashed. Must've been twenty seconds. Cold eyes. I could tell, even from that distance." she gestured to the point where this person was standing. "Really dark." she paused again, "So, I decided to confront him. I called the dogs and as I looked down to step from the shed, he must've turned, because when I looked up again, he was moving off. I followed, with the dogs trailing behind me, but when I got to the corner of the *leylandii* and looked down the drive, well, there was no-one."

"No-one?"

"No, it was like as soon as he was out of my sightline he evaporated – he must've sprinted off and then ducked into the rhodie by the Monkey Puzzle. We stood at the corner for a bit, with Nancy and Nelly doing their best impressions of the Hound of the Baskervilles while I held onto their collars. I didn't want them following this man, but also, I didn't want them to stop barking.

"Later, maybe five minutes or so, when we'd walked back up to the shed, and dogs had quietened, I heard a car engine – as if someone was driving off at speed. You know how you can hear stuff down here from the drivehead. I think he must've been parked up there. The dogs heard it too and started barking again."

"Bloody hell!" I put my arm around Sadie, "And what did he look like?"

"Oh, I don't know. Tall. Pale. Grey. He was wearing slacks, and a crew neck jumper, and a check shirt. Not much of a chin. Yes, and his eyes were watery, but intense.

As I said, cold."

"Age?"

"Difficult to say, but he's probably got ten or twenty on us."

"It's just so weird. Who'd do that – just stand there? And no attempt to speak or communicate?"

"No. No attempt at all." Sadie shook her head, "it was horrible. I didn't know what he wanted, and he just stood there. Assessing us, the shed, you know. A recce perhaps? Gave me the chills. Still does. I thought, maybe it's the guy from last time – you know the grey estate Kate and I saw? Same sort of assumption." she shook herself, "I mean, I am onsite all by myself. You are away. Anything could have happened."

"But it didn't. And the dogs …" I was trying to be comforting.

"I thought… I thought being here would be okay. Safe. You know. This is our place after all. And this visit. It undermines that."

"Well, maybe that was his intention."

"Well, it's worked."

Admonition the Thirty-sixth:
A Cup of Tea (with Cake)
Encourages Confidences

After that second unsettling visitation we remained very much *en garde*, particularly when I was off-site. Having the dogs was a comfort, even though they were extremely friendly. As I said to Sadie, people new to the site would have no idea that the Hounds were smiling and barking out of excitement to see them rather than warning them off.

But despite our caution and the dogs' enthusiasm, we learned very quickly that Dunans (and sometimes even its new inhabitants) excited a great deal of good-natured curiosity. There were locals who turned up to say hello, check we were okay and nose a bit, like Bogey or KP; then there were holidaymakers who wandered over the bridge in a state of bucolic wonder that such a place could ever exist, and who wanted to see as much as we'd allow; and finally, there were those who were connected to the place in some way. And it was often this latter group who were to provide us with both useful information and in the long run, a modicum of comfort.

I want to say they were driving a Metro. It was certainly a small car with good visibility – and Metros in their earlier incarnations were certainly that. It wasn't any bigger, and it was labouring. The engine I mean. That of course adds to my conviction – as Metros didn't have very big engines. And the engine, it rattled, as the driver struggled with the very uneven surface of our unimproved drive as well as, what I soon gathered was, a full complement of passengers.

I say all this because, as their electric-blue car emerged from behind the *leylandiis*, bounced past the turning to the red shed and then vanished behind the bank of overgrown *ponticum* towards the front of the castle, I had the distinct impression of the car's driver and three passengers. Through the large side windows I saw, as if caught by a telephoto lens, the shape of four statuesque ladies, each of a certain age, and each with a coloured rinse through their solidly coiffeured hair-dos. They were a veritable rainbow of thatch, crowded into what was evidently a very small space.

I don't know whether I imagined it, but the two ladies on the back seat had their handbags on their laps, their hands clasped over the bags' clasps and the handle loops over their wrists, lips pursed.

As I say, I was probably imagining it.

I stood on the step at the door of our ever-evolving chalet for a moment, possibly displaying a quizzical expression on my face given the vision I had just witnessed, or more likely, annoyance that the progress of my day was being interrupted – again.

I set my cup of tea down on the step – which was a mistake because both of the Bassets loved a cup of set-down-tea – and took myself off to greet our visitors, whoever they were.

As I rounded the courtyard turret to the front of the castle, I found aforesaid blue supermini disgorged of its cargo, and aforesaid cargo striding about in what I can only describe as a peremptory manner.

Now, before I go any further, I should mention that these ladies were well-turned out, as if for a Sunday drive prior to lunch, or even church. They had that air of smartness, of correctness that I in my dog-eared black polo shirt, worn brown corduroy cargo trousers and steel-toe-capped work-boots couldn't possibly contend with. However, sensing that this was an encounter rather than a curious sightseeing expedition, I ignored my sartorial disadvantage and jumped in, "Hello there! How can I help you?"

At my words the four span to face me, each with clutched handbag, each with eyes narrowed and lips pursed, "Help us?" the foremost lady, replied, in a voice that would have dropped a salvager of architectural relics at a hundred paces, "I am not sure you can." She looked me up and down with a certain amount of disdain, "Where is the owner?"

"I am the owner." I said, "Well, along with my wife, Sadie. I am Charles. Pleased to meet you all." I continued, smiling.

"Indeed." The foremost glanced at my hand disdainfully. I am not sure at this point any of them were convinced of the fact of my ownership either, "And did you allow *this* to happen?" She gestured at the ruined castle, a look of outrage on her face.

"Oh, by no means. We came here in March, well after the fire – which happened a couple of years ago, now."

"Oh?" said she of the foghorn voice.

"And what do you intend to do with it young man?" This was another of the ladies. She was slightly shorter than the loud one, with a more mollifying tone and a gentler hue of mauve for her rinse.

I smiled, "Oh, restore it and live in it. " I said airily.

"Oh well, that's a relief!" said the third, in a vibrant yellow, "What a relief! Isn't it Agnes?"

Of course, there was an Agnes. She was the fourth, and she nodded vigorously shaking her indigo coiffure, as the first enquired, "To live in?"

I eyed her, "Not really sure yet." I paused, and then asked, "What is your interest in the building?"

My primary interlocutor readied herself, but was beaten to an answer, if answer it was to be, by her second, who said, in a slightly breathless voice, "We used to live here!"

"You did! How wonderful! When?"

The second said, "Oh, in the fifties and sixties. We were all in service to the Fletchers at one time or another."

"You were? No wonder you were aghast to see the place now!"

"Indeed!" replied Foghorn, who I realised I could no longer keep thinking of as Foghorn and so introduced myself again and finally gained their names as Iris, Mathilda, Una, and Agnes, in that order.

Still seeing that Iris was not convinced, I invited them all in for a cup of tea and a chat with myself and Sadie.

That melted all reserve.

The ladies were particularly tickled with Sadie's knowledge of all things Fletcher. We learned much about life in the castle with the family and were later to find Iris and Agnes's names scribed into doors when we recovered them from the house.

We had several subsequent visits from the Metro girls, and each time I was quizzed at length on progress. The completion of the renovation of the house in 2007 was a great deal of comfort to all of them, particularly as we then had a *proper* kitchen to make tea in, and *proper* sofas on which to entertain our *very* distinguished guests.

Admonition the Thirty-seventh: Stop Smoking

A short encomium. The why, being the imminent arrival of the Eldest in the close confines of the red shed.

Plus, health.

Plus, Fagg.

The wheretofore, being the slow migration from prefabs, to rollies, to loooong rollies and the idea that a cigarette is only a substitute for one's mother's nipple.

Hmm. That last was enough to completely undermine the thought, "But what shall I do instead?"

In fact, the 'instead' happened to be countless teas.

And buns.

And biscuits.

And an ever-increasing waistband – from thirty-two to thirty-six.

But, on my thirty-fifth birthday my last drag was dragged, my last butt was flicked, and my remaining tobacco was disposed of.

I felt virtuous for about three hours.

Then desperate for a little more than three months.

And tempted for a further three quarters.

But by Eldest's first birthday I could properly claim to a feeling of nonchalance towards nicoteine and all those associated dependencies.

In life before Dunans, and Scotland, and, indeed, Sadie,

I worked with a venerable editor of books in Notting Hill. Sebastian his name was. And ironically, and coincidentally, his surname was Fagg. We'd stand at the bar of the Bonaparte imbibing a pint or two of Fuller's or somesuch (it was before I really made any choice beyond "a pint of bitter please") discussing issues of the day – me, some lackadaisical greenhorn with more opinion than experience, and Seb, a man of the world who had been everywhere at one time or another, with both the experience and the opinions to match. A strange pairing, but one brought together by the editorial management of what are termed promotional titles – mostly of illustrated non-fiction variety – *Great Train Disasters* anyone? Or even, *How to Make Paper Planes?* We would stand at the dark wood of the Victorian-era bar after work, and Seb would tell stories, impart wisdoms, and occasionally fire off the most outrageous one-liners, all the while sucking the life out of cigarette after cigarette. Fagg literally took the fag out of fags, injecting the whole process of smoking with a relish and vim I have rarely seen. Perennially single, and happy with it, I was charmed by this garrulous gentleman with his faded, threadbare suits, the shock of white hair, unruly, bushy eyebrows and yellow, nicoteined knuckles.

After all these years there is only one conversation with him, I remember in any detail. Perhaps that was because it was our first in the Princely or maybe it was just that I took it to heart, but it involved his time in America working for the marketing department of a very large tobacco company – a very, very large company, one that is still relatively well known.

"You see, Charlie, when I was there, in the early seventies, must've been, they'd been studying the effects of smoking for a while – the company itself I mean. For a decade and a half really. And the results were conclusive. Well, they'd been pretty convincing from the early sixties. They denied it over and over in public of course, but, in private they knew it was incontrovertible – try saying that after another pint, eh? Incontrovertible. And I am afraid, well, the stats showed that smoking cigarettes caused – causes – lung cancer. They knew it even as they put out ads for its apparent health benefits.

"It was truly tawdry and awful." Seb shook his head, "But their results were more granular than that, they knew – all of those companies knew really – that the data showed the deadly effects of smoking grew exponentially as people aged. They reckoned, privately, that if you stopped smoking before you hit your thirties, your lungs had a good chance of recovering – it was when you went beyond thirty-five that things really go to hell. Somehow, the body can no longer resist – the toxins build up to such a level that the carcinogenic action becomes all but inevitable." Seb stubbed out his cigarette, "Now, I'm a fifty-year-old man. I was in that industry. Party to that information. And I enjoy it a bit too fucking much to stop!" He shrugged, "Nicoteine has me in her thrall. I'd rather that than other much more damaging and expensive addictions, eh?" he grinned, clapped me on the arm, "Like the ladies!" He laughed uproariously, and followed up with, "Pint, old man?"

Eldest was born two months after my thirty-fifth birthday, the very birthday on which I rolled my last very large cigarillo and walked down the ravine path to the utmost southerly end of our policies, there to chuff away in silent, post-prandial satisfaction.

To be entirely honest dear reader, I did not finish that fag. That half-smoked rollie was flicked end-over-end into the swirling swollen waters of the Ruel in a glowing, spiralling arc. Evidently, I'd listened too hard to Seb, and only, finally had had the gumption to stop when both the nominated age came upon me, and fatherhood beckoned. Beforehand I tried – to stop I mean – but never quite made it. Always I think, I'd previously used Seb's words to provide me with an excuse, a reason to procrastinate, to subvert my impulse to throw the damn things away for good. Not that I blame Seb. I think the truth I am highlighting here is that perhaps, sometimes, I am unduly influenced by an off-hand remark, or a well-turned story – I allow them to steer me, or guide me, consciously or subconsciously.

Is that a common trait? I am not sure, but what I do know is that the opposite is true also.

When a relation remarked, "Oh, when we heard you'd bought a castle, well, oh, how we laughed! We all thought you were quite potty!" that was enough to fix me on my intent to restore Dunans.

And then, when later one of the Offal Brethren declared, "I am going to press the big red 'Fuck it' button and go for you and do whatever it takes to bring you down." that was all it took for me to dig in and persist.

To reheat the metaphor of the fourth admonition, sometimes influences seem like random eddies guiding the steps you take. At others, I think, you step on despite the prevailing current, knowing that your certainty will carry you to your destination.

Or at least, hoping that you know that.

Admonition the Thirty-eighth: Stand Your Ground

T he call came in on a Sunday evening a month or so after we'd moved into the red shed. We'd been enjoying a quiet early supper in front of the TV because we'd finally managed to get our Sky box working.

And if you are wondering why we were not able to view normal terrestrial TV, then I would gently point out that often those at the end of dog-legged glens with no sightline to so-called civilisation, are often unable to access the relevant UHF signal.

"Hello, Charles speaking."

"Hello, Mr. Dixon-Spain, this is your neighbour." The voice had a slight Scottish burr, but only slight. It was middle-class, without much weight to it. Not quite nasal, but as I later learned, it had that tendency, particularly when crossed, or petulant.

"Ah, hello there! How good of you to call." I mouthed to Sadie, "It's our neighbour, *Haslet*!"

There was no pre-amble, "So, by now you will have realised you have bought a property with lots of problems – and I don't mean the roof Mr. Dixon-Spain. I mean your boundaries. Indeterminate boundaries and disintegrating march fences. In addition, you don't have any rights to water and none for your electricity supply either. You also have the temerity to lock the gate. You lock it!"

Many folks would have put the phone down. Others

might have launched into a tirade. I didn't: with such a preamble, such an aggressive opening, I felt it might be useful to extract as much information as possible from the caller before losing my temper. I had to do this, I knew, without agreeing to or in any way condoning any of his outlandish statements. It would be difficult, but I was game.

I responded, "Indeed? You seem exercised, perhaps you'd like to explain these things to me a little?"

"Well, to begin with your water apparatus sits on my land and takes water from my stream and I do not give, have never given, will never give permission for you to take it from there."

"Will you not? Is not my right to take water from that burn part of my deeds?"

"Oh no. I know those deeds. I wrote them you see. I did. And what I meant ... my meaning was that you were to take your water from the *historical* source – the source that the Fletchers took their water from when they lived at the castle. From the dam. Not the present illegally installed apparatus. The people, the erstwhile hoteliers you bought from, they installed that. They did. They overstepped the mark. They got that handyman, you know, that idiot Gregory and his friend, the boy-racer, to install it. He knew it was illegal – in fact, they all knew it was an illegitimate installation. Those thousand-litre tanks, they may be on your land – the rest not at all. On mine."

"Is that so? Well, as far as I am concerned that supply, that apparatus, that is the water supply. That's what the deeds say. Not the dam, which is unusable. The present apparatus is where we take our water from and will continue to do so."

"The deeds do not allow that! You are wrong! Wrong! And your electricity. You take electricity across my land on those overheads. And I am not having it. You do not have my permission."

"Do I not?"

"No. You don't have rights and I can prove it!"

"Can you? How interesting."

"Yes, I should think so. And your boundaries Mr. Dixon-Spain, your boundaries. They are wrong. That parcel to the south isn't yours. They should never have sold it to you, those infernal hoteliers. No rights to it. At. All."

"Ah, I take it you are referring to McGuffy's copse?"

There was a pause, as if perturbed that I was so well informed, "Yes, that's the one."

"Well, McGuffy still owns it. The way he tells it, you tried to sell it to the hoteliers."

"Nonsense. Stuff and nonsense. I would never act in such an underhand manner."

"Would you not?"

"No, as you may have gathered it was the hoteliers who acted in underhand ways. Taking water without permission, taking electricity without permission, trying to claim land from Mr. McGuffy."

"I am not sure how I was to gather all of this. All I know is that I had a reputable firm of solicitors convey the property, and they assured me that all services were as seen and also, there were no disputes."

"More fool you then."

"So you say. What evidence can you provide to confirm what you say is true, that there is a dispute and that its historical?"

"I don't need evidence; I drew up the deeds. My intention trumps all."

"Does it indeed?" Sadie handed me a beer, a bowl of popcorn and gestured for me to go and make myself comfortable. I'd been pacing back and forth in our tiny galley kitchen getting in the way.

"Moreover, there's the issue of the drivehead."

"The drivehead? That's an issue? Is it? Really?"

"Well, you seem to think that you own more of the drivehead than you actually do."

"Is that so?"

"Ah yes you have but two and a half metres from the lefthand side of the verge there, all of the way up to where the drivehead issues onto the main road. No more. You cannot claim any more than that. And the small standing stone?"

"What about it?"

"Well, that is on my land, so I own it. It is not yours. Never will be." He paused for a quick breath and then continued in his rant, "And the bridge. Well, you have taken on a very large restoration project there!"

I nodded, "You are not wrong there. If I remember correctly maintenance and repair is by usage, and we intend to ensure that that structure is maintained. We will have to ensure we apportion costs appropriately."

"We, Mr. Dixon-Spain? We?" he chuckled – he actually chuckled, "I think you will find that there is no 'We' about it ..."

At this I finally bridled. I was very aware of my rights as landowner, and also my obligations. Any neglect of a listed structure can be prosecuted by Historic Environment Scotland in the criminal courts. In other words, if I did not take my responsibilities seriously, I might be fined, or worse! "No, I am very sure you have obligations to us ... I have read the deeds with great care."

"... you see until you stop taking water and electricity from my land there will be no discussion on other matters. No discussion at all."

"That seems a little high-handed!"

"High-handed! High-handed? No, I think you will find I am standing my ground, and you will also find that I do not back down. Ever."

I couldn't help myself, I guffawed.

"Funny Mr. Dixon-Spain? I think not."

I could see Sadie was mystified. A bit of audible exposition was indicated to keep her up to speed, "So, let me get this straight. You question our deed-given right to take water, electricity, and access as we presently do. Further you cast doubt on our boundaries and our ability to maintain the bridge which we own, and which you, as owner of the sawmill ..."

"Steadings!" I moved the handset away from my ear a little, grimacing. Sadie's face showed a mixture of amazement and surprise.

"... have an obligation to contribute to. And you won't contribute to any maintenance program until we have changed our service and access arrangements."

"Exactly."

"Hmm. Well, we have reached an impasse then. We will maintain our right to take water and power as we do and will not allow any person or organisation to compromise our services –" There was a spluttering down the phone, "... and we will maintain the bridge as necessary and bill you accordingly."

"Well, you can try."

"As I say, we are at an impasse."

"It certainly looks like it."

"And to ensure you understand me, unless you can absolutely prove what you say, which I am sure you cannot, we will not be conceding any part of our position. You will find we are just as obdurate and unwilling to step backward as you claim to be."

There was a pause.

Admonition the Thirty-ninth: Know When to End a Phonecall

The phone line crackled. I found myself wondering what his next step would be. In the end he surprised me by changing tack, "There is of course another matter Mr. Dixon-Spain we should discuss. You see, I have certain documents that you, as the new owner of the castle, might be interested in?"

"Might I?"

"Well, indeed. You may not be aware that the bridge you now own and have responsibility for was designed and built in 1815 for John Fletcher by the eminent Victorian engineer ..."

"Yes, yes, Thomas Telford."

The man harrumphed, "And the castle was remodelled by ..."

"Andrew Kerr, Edinburgh architect – yes, yes we have read the relevant listings, spoken to the relevant authorities – we are aware ..."

"... Well in my possession are certain documents pertaining to the building of bridge and castle."

"Ah, so you do still have the original plans for the bridge and the castle – this is what I had been given to understand, but it's good to know that information is correct."

"Indeed. So, these are wonderful original artefacts. Deeply interesting and of course very valuable."

I sighed, put my hand over the receiver and whispered to Sadie, "Very valuable apparently!" My wife shook her head in despair – we both knew what was coming.

I returned my attention to the call, "… we would be more than willing to pass these documents on for a small consideration."

"Small? Oh, and what sort of figure were you thinking?"

I could hear the self-satisfied smile lift his voice into a slightly higher register, "Oh, I don't know … but I have them insured for twenty-five thousand pounds, so special are they considered by our insurers."

"Twenty-five thousand pounds!? Is that all?" As he spluttered down the phone Sadie jumped up in horror. I waved at her to hold on – I was determined to enjoy myself, "I expected you to mention a six-figure sum. Twenty-five undersells the value of these documents surely?" Sadie waved at me in despair, "These documents are of critical importance to the listing of all these buildings – they are the validating paperwork – the historical artefacts which will unlock grant-funding, the involvement of the national agencies we have been talking about. And that's just their effect – as genuine, contemporaneous papers they are priceless to any owner of the castle, but most especially the bridge – which you'll agree is of national, if not international importance. No, believe me when I say, a six-figure sum is entirely justified …"

"Well …"

I could feel him struggling with himself, and though I didn't know what he looked like I imagined him pale and sweaty now, trying to imagine how he could get me back to those financially sunny uplands of six figures. I continued, "I am guessing that these documents were given to you during your purchase of the castle? And that the Fletchers wanted the papers to remain with the buildings?"

"Indeed."

"Can I ask why you didn't hand these papers on to the folks who purchased from you."

Haslet harrumphed again, "Well, frankly I didn't trust them. They were – are – *nouveau riche* – and not that *riche* as it turned out." He chuckled to himself in an ugly way. "Being *nouveau*, they were unused to the idea that our built heritage is held in trust to future generations." His voice became hoarse with dramatised anger "... and look what happened. They burned the place down. Lost all that history. Awful. Awful. Probably criminal I'd say. Insurance job I am sure of it. And all of it, all of their actions, well, they vindicated my decision to withhold the documents."

"Oh, I see."

"Of course, you do. It was obvious from the first that they were headed for the rocks in one form or another. So yes, perfectly legal, and proper for myself and my wife to retain the papers. Perfectly."

"Well, whether it was legal or proper remains to be seen – it certainly wasn't ethical, was it?"

"And what would you know about ethical Mr. Dixon-Spain? What would you know?"

I ignored the question, "So, I have a proposal, with regard to the documents which you hold." I winked at Sadie.

"You do?"

"My proposal is that you will withdraw your claims on water, electricity, access, boundaries *et cetera, et cetera* – all those things – and once you have, you then hand over the original historical documents that should have remained in the possession of the owners of the castle and bridge, as the Fletchers requested." I paused.

"And?"

"And nothing."

"Nothing? No financial consideration for these valuable documents and rights?" He scoffed.

"Well, yes, the consideration is that you remain in good

standing with myself and my wife who, after all, own the bridge over which you access your property."

"Good standing? Good standing!? Do you know what you can do with your good standing Mr. Dixon-Spain?"

And there, dear reader, I withdrew the receiver from my ear and gently pressed the red button which ended the call. Thereafter, I took a long draft of my slightly less than cool but still refreshing beer. I looked at my hand which was shaking, but only slightly. "So, darling, I don't think I liked him one bit. I might go further, and say I positively disliked him. Additionally, I think, given his tone, and his vocabulary, we have now probably identified the hanger of the egregious signage we spotted last summer. I am fairly sure also, that that man," I nodded at the phone, "was the wielder of the alkathin-cutting hacksaw. Obviously, I can't prove any of it, but he's certainly got the attitude, and therefore plenty of motivation."

"Lovely! I also got the impression that he is not for backing down on anything?"

"No. I am not really clear on his legal grounds for insisting there is an issue. He didn't really explain, he just insisted he was correct. Nor could I really ascertain why he was immediately antagonistic."

"I wonder ..." Sadie paused, thinking, "... you know that morning – when you were taking Mike back, and I was here by myself. And you came back, and I was a bit shaken? You know? *That* day... *That* encounter?"

"Ah yeah, the tall man."

"Yes. That horrid-looking man and his horrid energy."

"Yes, the one who just stood and watched."

"Yeah him. I think that was him… I suppose it was the assumption of the intruder – that he could just turn up, that no-one should be here ... and that when there was, he considered it an intrusion on his fiefdom. You know that thing about just staring when he saw me at the door. It's the same sort of ... profile let's say, as the man on the phone, from what I could hear."

"Maybe ..."

"Look, that day left me feeling like this. Wrong-footed. Uncomfortable. Angry. And vulnerable Charlie. Vulnerable. It's evidently what he wants. To scare us away. To get rid of us."

I nodded, "Well frankly, that phone call," I glanced at the receiver which I still held in my hand, "has only made me more determined not to give ground – in any way."

"I agree – but what the hell did we do to deserve such a neighbour?"

Admonition the Fortieth:
Further Advice on Dealing
with the Midge

That first year, in the hut with single-glazed windows of approximate fit, without airlock (also known as the porch) for the shaking out of insect-life from hair, clothes and dog, without any through-breeze onsite of any kind, the midges were sanity-threatening awful. If I have latterly called the castle a glorified mouse-breeding box, then that's because the rash-filled paddock next to the Red Shed, with its sundry hollows, its deeply scored quad bike tracks, the miscellaneous divots, and other depressions, all causing the retention of water to the point walking in it required waders, was similarly termed the midge-breeding box. We identified this area as the main midge infestation problem and that was where we focussed our attention.

To wage a successful war against the midge one needs to remember two things: first, this is a long-term campaign and second, there are no short-term solutions. You'll also need to remember two further things: first, as alluded to in our very first swarming encounter (*see* "Admonition the Twenty-ninth"), midges cannot withstand a breeze of more than one point five metres per second, they are literally blown away, and second, they are crepuscular.

You can walk a swarm off – they literally cannot keep

up. If you spot several Scots in a field having an agricultural chat, they'll not be leaning on a five-bar gate (mostly because three of the five bars are rotten, and the top is so patched with scraps of kindling that its actually quite uncomfortable to lean against) they'll be walking in an ever-increasing spiral. Obviously, they'll not want a decreasing spiral because the Pygmy flies will then end up concentrating in the correct space. Also, these voluble West Coast farmers – because, believe me, they can be very voluble – will avoid their livestock. Livestock generally have their own domestic swarm, a colony of midges, who for the summer describe a cloud or halo around their chosen beast. There are also ticks, but that is another matter altogether.

Now concerning the crepuscular element of the equation (and here I should admit that Eliot's "Fire Sermon" is the only reason I had any notion as to what this poly-syllabic term meant before the advent of midges in my life) the reasons midges are dusk and dawn-favouring are two-fold, first, the lack of sun. They, like moles, mice and marmots do not like direct sunlight. Well, mice might, but they prefer cover from marauding predators than full sunlit exposure. Not having researched the subject, I am not sure why midges don't like sunlight, but (vast) experience shows this to be the case. Second, at dusk and dawn, any air movement generally falls away, making reaching an objective actually possible. There may of course be a third reason. Midges feed on blood. Any blood. They are not fussy. Human, deer, coo, sheep, dog, cat. At dawn and dusk these creatures are not wont to rush about madly, they slow, they prepare for the onset of night or begin the process of waking. The midge prey is therefore not moving at more than one-point-five metres per second and is therefore vulnerable to a savaging.

How is it you may ask that such tiny creatures can find their prey with such alacrity? Midges are attracted initially to the carbon dioxide their prey emits, then by movement, colour and odour. Finally, once a midge finds prey it emits a pheromone which attracts other midges.

It may be the pheromone which finally persuaded us that midge magnets weren't for us. Either that, or the thought of using a can of gas every couple of months to produce a constant stream of carbon dioxide to attract midges. While we awaited the effect of the changes we began soon after that tortured evening of the soul, we caved in and invested in such a magnet.

Now, quite apart from our understandable reservations, as rehearsed above, the midge magnet ended up being entirely unsuccessful, not because it didn't work, but because of my inability to remember to check the gas canister on a regular basis. And empty the nets of midges as they neared full. And actually, get the magnet lit. Once I'd managed to remember to check the canister and see that it'd been empty for some time – given the deliquescence of midges in midge-net – I'd then have to get to Strachur to replace the canister. Only to have to order a canister because I was the only person using that particular type of valve. Then, I'd forget to remember to return the following week once the gas supplier had delivered said preferred type – remember a further week later and manage to buy the last canister of the preferred type, with the smallest capacity, given that four other households "... had just decided in the last week to give these wee midge-magnet-thingies a try!"

No, midge magnets weren't the solution, not at Dunans, not with our infestation, not with my record of replenishment and maintenance. There is a far-flung corner of a shed where several hundred-pounds-worth of kit moulders, paying tribute to our commitment to rid ourselves of midges and also, to our eventual success.

That first long, bitey summer we, and various members of our family and many friends, spent hours upon hours brush-cutting rashes, felling *leylandii* and filling divots, tracks and pits found in that field. There were countless bonfires of brash, rakings of soggy hay and well-earned six-o'clock beers – obviously in range of our constantly spinning floor fans, smokey barbecue and cigarette smoke. We made inroads that year, but in the long-term, over the three or four years following, we reduced the incidence of midge deluges markedly, such that now, it is only of passing interest when we have a bad day. My paltry efforts, along with mighty shifts by folk like VBF, Chris, Stuart, Min and Tino, have led to policies in which it is possible to picnic, or to barbecue, in comparative comfort with only an occasional surfeit of airborne bitery.

We do still dress our open windows in organza though… and practice a lights-out policy during late-May, June, and July … and utilise floor and desk-mounted fans.

Admonition the Forty-first: Obstinacy Isn't Always A Good Thing

Maybe it was because the shed was raised on a platform, perhaps it was because I'd ordered single glazing. It could have been that the insulation we'd used was not properly applied, or maybe that we really should have forgone the four inches of space a conventional insulation solution would have taken. Perhaps our radiators should have been doubles, or that our pipe runs could have been somehow shorter, or even maybe we should have used a pressurized system with microbore copper. It could have been that all of our ceilings should have been dropped to the height of the A-frame crossbeam, or that thicker curtains and deeper rugs would have made a difference. I can say with certainty now that the stove we'd bought was not big enough for the job, and also that I had no idea of how much wood, peat, or coal a multifuel stove could go through between September and April – because that is how long the season is, usually.

That winter, our first at the head of the glen, in comparative isolation and with no idea what was in store for us, was pretty arduous. I discovered for example, that *leylandii*, as felled that summer, when dry, burnt in seconds. But there wasn't much that was actually dry, and actually seasoned. The fallen branches of our Monkey Puzzle provided longer-lasting warmth even when wet – although we didn't much like the fragrance which reminded me in particular of Elm. The *rhododendron ponticum* we progressively cleared from the environs of the shed that winter burned very well once lit. But actually, lighting it was a bore. Like the Monkey Puzzle it was really quite a calorific fuel, even when wet and unseasoned. We had some ash, which was great, but we only had a little. We took a delivery of apparently dry, seasoned wood, which was nothing of the sort. I went out with a trailer and picked up some logs from a farmer, but that took a day to retrieve and process, and heated us for only three. We gathered windfall from the woods surrounding us. We used all the offcuts from the building work we'd already undertaken. The problem was that I couldn't keep up, nor would the stove stay in all night, and despite evidence to the contrary supplied by Sadie, I would not concede that either was insoluble. Each day I would spend two, or three, or four hours winning fuel for the next – clearing, or logging, or splitting, or carrying. And each morning one of us would spend half an hour clearing and re-lighting a stove that seemed reluctant to draw, to keep alight, to heat the radiators as much as we needed. Whether I would admit it at the time, it was a rude introduction to the realities of heating a house without using conventional, more capital-intensive methods – like an oil- or gas-fired boiler.

By Christmas Sadie had quite reasonably reached the end of her tether with our damp, cold, living conditions.

So, without any concession to the lesson reality was trying to teach me, I made the decision to do something radical.

At the top of the paddock there was a Scot's Pine which had come down the previous winter. This, I thought, would be an ideal tree to cut up and win prodigious amounts of timber from over the next few months. I'd already taken the branches from what remained of the canopy, so I knew this was well-seasoned and worthwhile timber.

However, I had several obstacles to overcome. First, was a fourteen-inch bar on my Makita chainsaw, meaning each round would take two cuts to separate from the log, second was my haphazard approach to sharpening chainsaw chains. I found it quite difficult to sharpen them, and to make sure the sharpening was the same on both sides.

The last obstacle was actually getting the cut timber down from the site of the fallen tree to our wood store.

I thought the first two were trivial in comparison to the last.

Now, Boris, our venerable Disco, and our only road-legal vehicle, was a four-by-four, and therefore, I thought, I should be able to get it up the hill to the lumber. I knew enough to wait until we'd had some dry days, and also, until midday when the winter sun had dried-off most of the frosty dew. I also knew to use low ratio and to maintain momentum. For three hours I tried. I spread gravel. I used sarking as ramping. I used jute sacks for grip. I tried snow chains. I managed to get a fifth of the distance required.

I gave up.

But only on Boris.

It occurred to me that I might roll twelve-inch-thick rounds, cut from the twenty-four-inch diameter log, down the hill. I'd just have to roll it across as well as down – like a tyre from a car.

Couldn't be *that* difficult, I thought.

The idea worked to an extent. With a newly-sharpened chain I cut a reasonable line through the downhill side. Unfortunately, when it came to cutting uphill side two things became apparent: the first was that the chain was sufficiently blunted by the first cut that it would take twice the time to go through this side and second, that somehow the chain wanted to cut down away to the right. Resharpening was indicated.

By the time I'd re-sharpened the chain, refilled the saw with fuel and walked back up to the site dusk was well on the way. I cut for another five minutes. I could feel the new round vibrate with me as I cut. It was about to drop. I didn't want the round to drop without me being able to control it. I sawed for thirty seconds more, and as I saw the top edge come slightly away from the log I stopped. I dropped to my knees and tried to work out how much of a connection there was still left. It looked substantial. I wiped my forehead thinking. I fired up the chainy again. Except it didn't fire. It was being temperamental. I tried again. Nothing.

Frustrated I tried to kick the round loose.

There was a crack. "A-ha" I thought and kicked the round again.

This time there was a tearing sound and the round lurched to the ground, and as it did so, the bark started peeling away.

I saw the danger immediately and tried to grab the loosened wood, to stop it immediately rolling down the hill, except that in my haste I hadn't realised that by detaching the round I had inadvertently lightened the load on the main log itself, and that thirty-foot long stump was starting to revert to its original vertical. As the tree rose like some silvan Lazarus it caught my elbow, lifted my arm, and bounced me sideways.

As I toppled, the round leaped away from me, gaining momentum on its downward trajectory even as I subsided into the long rashes and the remaining trunk was forced upright by its huge root ball.

Winded, bruised and somewhat dismayed I lay for a moment staring up at the overcast sky and resurrected tree stump. In the distance there was an ominous crash, and then another.

I levered myself upright. The round was nowhere to be

seen, but in the half-light, I could see a thin tongue of blonde wood quivering a hundred or so yards downhill – the round had smashed through the bank of rhododendrons that lined our march stream. I groaned. It was too much and too late. I'd check things in the morning.

It was a measure of my sheer bone-headedness that even this experience did not alter my conviction that I would be able to sort our heating out. Indeed, on discovering the round had landed in a deep pool in the burn and was therefore virtually unrecoverable, I resolved to fell the Lazarus pine instead.

Luckily for all of us Christmas intervened, and with it our first child's due-date. We bought dry firewood from the Filly in Strachur, a Christmas tree from the Scouts and postponed the issue of my intransigence until after Sadie had given birth.

Admonition the Forty-second: Acknowledge that Sometimes Temporary Can Be *Too* Temporary

Eldest arrived the day before Hogmanay that first year, and entirely changed my perspective on everything, not least our living arrangements.

Now don't get me wrong, this was a deeply joyful moment for both of us personally, but within four hours of the birth of our firstborn I realised, despite wanting to stay with them, I had to get back to Dunans, to ready the shed, to warm it up before the forecast sub-zero temperatures started doing unspeakable things to our plumbing and ruined my family's homecoming. So, as soon as they were settled and comfortable, I kissed my wife and my child, promised I'd be back on the morrow, and ordered a taxi.

It was eleven o'clock in the evening, the day before Hogmanay. It took forty minutes for the cab to arrive. The car was a grubby white, and every panel was scuffed or dinked or stained. The windscreen had an eight-inch crack on the passenger side, and the headlights were a dim yellow, behind a season's-worth of salty grime. I sighed, confirmed this was my cab with the driver, and levered myself into the passenger seat.

The ride back had an hallucinatory quality.

Despite the fact that I hadn't slept for around twenty-four hours, and I was struggling to say anything coherent as I sat beside him, it seemed my driver, Jimmy, was intent on both delivering a lecture on the rivalry between Rangers and Celtic over the course of his entire taxi-driving career and ensuring that he never drove in a straight-line. In the latter case, whether his non-linear steering technique was because one tyre or the other was soft, or he had some sort of stigmata, or the steering column was faulty, I am not sure, but each time he corrected the car's course it resulted in a further curve with seemingly no prospect of achieving equilibrium – otherwise known as a straight line. This slow bounce from side to side of the road – and I do mean *road* rather than *lane* – as we lifted up and over the Rest and Be Thankful, along Loch Fyneside and through the forests to home, became increasingly perilous as we ventured deeper and deeper into the lonely darkness of the hills and the temperature dropped further and further. There was little other traffic, particularly once we'd turned off the '83 and onto the Fyneside road – this welcome as every pair of oncoming headlights set my heart racing.

The constant slow swerve was also making me feel deeply nauseous.

By the time we reached the Leanachd we were down to minus four and there were suggestions of fish-tailing at every correction Jimmy made to the momentum of his battered Toyota Camry. I'd taken to staring fixedly into the deep darkness of the forests we passed trusting that my new status of parent would protect me from death by parabolic driving. By now it was gone half past one, and despite the nausea I was increasingly anxious about the state of our plumbing in the unheated red shed.

I watched as familiar gates, and familiar fences, and familiar trees slid by. When we passed the dirty sign announcing *Glendaruel* I whimpered in relief. By now the nausea was sitting in my clavicle, a noxious, complacent toad, goading my saliva glands into action. Four miles to go. I was gulping reflexively. This was not helped by the long curves of the road which seemed to increase the frequency of Jimmy's parabolic progress. His long soccer narrative faltered as he glanced across at me. Evidently, he didn't like what he saw and his hands gripped the wheel more firmly, he muttered, "Aye, it's dark oot here, is it not?"

"No streetlamps," I muttered rather lamely.

"Aye, well, and very faint road markings too. Quite the hazard."

"Aye" I said, "We're nearly there."

"That's good. Hey, are you alright – do y'want me to stop?"

I nodded urgently, not wanting to open my mouth.

Three hundred metres from the drivehead, just before Dunans Cottage we slid to a halt. And even before we were fully stationary, I flung the door open and leaned out. I was not sick, but I lay over the car sill for a full minute before the chill night air and heavy breathing calmed my crisis. Without a word I righted myself and then levered legs out to stand. I looked around. "Black as a badger's hat." I muttered.

"Sorry?" asked Jimmy.

"Oh, it's alright, you can leave me here," I said, "… it's not far. I'll walk."

"Oh okay. Are you sure? It's very fucking dark!" He seemed relieved.

I rummaged in my pockets, looking for cash. I found my keyring torch first, and then my wallet. Relieved in both cases, I leant through the passenger window and handed him the cash, "Thanks Jimmy, much appreciated."

"Nae problemo." He tucked the notes in a cubby hole, and with chuckle asked, "If you don't mind me asking, what do ye want to live the way out here in bumfuck nowhere fae?"

I smiled haggardly, "No I don't mind at all…." I

paused, "It's something I have been asking myself since we left Glasgow." He laughed, "Let's say, I am not sure I knew what I was letting myself in for."

"Ha! Well, it takes all kinds – as ma' grandmammy would say, 'Yer a hardy chiel, so ye are!' Good luck to ye!"

With a cheery wave and a U-turn in which he bounced his tired old saloon over the frozen eight-inch-high verge on the opposite side of the road. I swear there was no curve in his course as he chugged up the hill.

I turned and twisted the tiny torch on. I was wearing only a light jacket and the cold had banished the last suggestion of car-sickness, so I jogged up the road and then the two-hundred-and-fifty yards down the drive to the shed feeling that I'd made a lucky escape, but also concerned that I'd be too late to save our plumbing.

The shed was a fridge by the time I made it back – colder, if anything, than the frosty air outside. The bed was a freezing mound of duvet and pillow, there was a rime of ice on the water in the sink and condensation had frozen on the inside of the windows. It did not look good.

I lit the fire using the last of the firelighters, piled the remainder of my kindling with the smokeless fuel on top and remained crouched over the grate for the next half an hour as the tiny conflagration caught and eventually warmed me. Finally, after an hour I closed the top vent and relaxed a bit.

But only a bit. Part of me was still listening for the telltale sound of trickling water, that by turns, or rather by progressive melting, was sure to become a pressurized flood.

Notwithstanding the idea of a burst pipe and having toasted my wife and my new child with a Jura, eaten a flapjack and wrapped myself in a blanket, I promptly fell asleep on the sofa.

I woke at four in the morning. The room was barely warm. My breath plumed in front of me. I was frozen.

Nothing unusual in that, for winter at Dunans that is. But, somewhere, out of sight, in the deep black gloom beyond the bare bulb of the side-light, I could hear the trickle and drip of water.

As you can imagine I swore, loudly but briefly, and then quietened myself and set to listen and track the leak. It seemed to be coming from the back quarter where kitchen and bathroom were located. This was potentially very bad news. I retrieved my big torch from the hook on the back of the front door and began to look for the leak.

Here in the darkest watch of the night, at a time when happiness should be overwhelming, when life should feel its best, the fact was our existence in a wooden box, in the dark end of the glen, in a frost pocket, was hardly bearable.

In the bathroom I found the source of the sound of water. Knowing it would be cold, knowing we'd be away, knowing what a bust pipe could mean to our marginal existence, Sadie'd left the cold tap of the bath running just enough to prevent the worst happening. I sat on the end of the bath staring at the trickling water: Sadie had been able to think this through as she was experiencing increasingly painful contractions, while we waited for the ambulance to arrive to take us to Glasgow. I shook my head in the torchlit bathroom in disbelief and admiration.

Tomorrow, before I left for Glasgow, I would make a plan which included a bigger stove, buying lots of fuel, and perhaps, some electric heaters too.

I left the tap open, refilled the fire and finally, gratefully, went to bed.

Admonition the Forty-third: Recognise a "Gate" When It Appears

In the grey light of a late January afternoon, as we approached the end of our first full year at Dunans, we returned, as we would several times that year following, to a scene of utter devastation at our drive head. This was to be the start proper of the "Gate-gate" of "Admonition the Twenty-seventh" as described in *How to Restore a Castle: Part One*.

The gate was unhinged and lying across the track, the closing post stood twenty degrees off vertical, with various chainsaw tracks across its base. The hinge post had been definitively felled, with the almost white circle of its stump seemingly hovering an inch or so above the black mud of the trampled ground. Our bin housing had been torn down, with its walls violently disassembled and strewn across the driver's-side verge. And besides that, our temporary post box had been rendered unusable by the simple expedient of having its lid ripped off.

I stopped the car, turned off the engine and stared blankly at the carnage.

It was, in that moment, impossible to feel anything. We'd returned from a lovely time away with family expecting to settle into a Sunday evening of preparation for the week ahead. A comfortable, domestic, safe routine.

And here, at our drivehead, in our space, at the entrance to our home, we were presented with chaos and vandalism. This was more than a discovery of sabotaged water months after the fact, more than disputatious phone calls taking issue directly and specifically: this spoke to an immediacy, a directness, which in the dusk, in the falling light and gathering shadow, was both deeply unsettling and, of course, enraging.

Being the master of understatement, I muttered a few well-chosen epithets under my breath.

"Quite." said Sadie, "Oh Charlie, this is intolerable. I mean we knew some folk weren't keen on us being here, but this?"

"Agreed. If it is the neighbours that is …"

"No, well it could be vandals."

"Or some of the architectural salvage crews we had heard talk of. Whoever. Beyond the pale."

"No, Charlie that is to understate it. This is criminal damage."

Behind us Eldest stirred, reminding us we required to get back to the Red Shed sharpish. I leapt out and cleared the track to allow us to drive down. I flung the gate to the side making quite a sound in the chill silence. As it landed there was a further crash and a yip. Then another flurry of movement. Something was scarpering noisily through the thick *rhododendron*. It was difficult to tell what the creature was, but I thought that bark sounded like fox. I turned back to the car, still fulminating.

Later, once Sadie and offspring were settled with a lit fire and warm comforting drink, I went back up to make good. Dusk was falling rapidly so I'd snaffled the big rechargeable torch – the one that shone a thousand candles across any scene.

The gate I'd thrown to the side of the drive was still serviceable – they'd only bent its bottom two rungs. Evidently, whoever it was hadn't thought to bring a hack saw.

As I righted the gate by the felled hinge post I noted the sopping sawdust arced across and down the track. I decided it would have been a quick cut, and also that it would've been unlikely that anyone would have remarked on what was going on, even if they had passed during the cut. I slung the post to the side to reveal in the torchlight another bright slash of white. Puzzled, I bent down and picked up several sopping envelopes, all soaked through and unreadable.

It looked as if a couple of the envelopes had been ripped opened.

I stared at the night sky and swore.

This new intrusion spoke to the perpetrator's mentality, of their disregard for us and for the law when it came to us. It seemed to me that they had othered us, but what that othering consisted of, I had no idea. If you don't know someone personally, it is really very easy to make assumptions – particularly denigrating ones. Mostly othering happens around ethnicity, or nationality, or even religion, and of the three, I had no idea which applied, because I had no indication as to what they thought they knew about us – beyond our purchase of the property.

As I mulled things over, feeling more and more disheartened, I continued to look around. It occurred to me that the drivehead scene was missing something.

It took a moment to recognise that there was no green Argyll & Bute branded wheelie-bin standing or lying alongside our postbox. With a growing sense of dread, I remembered we'd left it full of rubbish, ready for uplift, before the weekend.

Where was it?

I stilled, thinking.

And in my stillness, I heard soft movement in the rhododendron undergrowth.

And then, as I concentrated, I realised I could I hear the faint noise of chewing.

With a groan I walked over to the closing post and the

side of the drive. I parted the head-high rhododendron and shone my torch down.

It took a moment for me to comprehend what I was seeing.

There, in a small clearing was the long wide rectangle of the bin, its top open on the ground, angled towards me like some food-encrusted tongue. And in the aperture of the bin-mouth, a pair of yellow eyes. For the longest moment we stared at one another, the unblinking feral pair stilling my electric cyclops. Then, the pair blinked, and broke the brief hypnosis. With a flurry of movement and a cacophony of skittering as its nails tried to gain purchase on the bin lid, the fox was gone, long brush bouncing after it as it sprang into the darkness beyond the strafe of my torchlight.

Fig. 2 – The Old Dog Fox

I held the bright beam of my torch after it, as if the light could penetrate the deep green of the woodland understorey. Slowly I came to realise that even though the fox had scarpered, I could still hear the munching.

I altered the angle of the torch and scanned over the clearing. As I did so, the light fell on two-week's worth of rubbish. Our rubbish. Yoghurt pots, nappies, teabags, packaging. And in the middle of all that was a tatty old dog fox watching me beadily, his jaws working over something unmentionable.

Another disbelieving pause.

I yelled "Go on!" and gestured at him.

Another beat, to make sure I was serious, then he turned, and loped off, in the direction his mate had taken.

Both slope and vulpine attention rendered the clear-up dangerous, noisome, and time-consuming.

An hour and I'd recovered three-quarters.

Another hour, and I'd cleared all visible materials. I returned the next day, in daylight, for a final sweep, as well as to repair the damage inflicted on our sundry drivehead installations.

I realised that the presence of rubbish gave me a timeline for the vandalism. We'd departed on Thursday afternoon, and the rubbish uplift was scheduled for the early morning on the Friday. Our perpetrators had evidently made their move on the Thursday evening. Furthermore, because their vandalism occurred so soon after we had left, I could only conclude that we were being watched, or that, if not watched *per se*, the beginnings of our journey had been marked, or remarked upon.

Over the next months we found that absence truly makes the vandal try harder. They repeated their nastiness several more times: while we were away for weekends, sometimes just for a night or even once, just an afternoon.

Eventually mail was delivered to the house, bins brought to the top as needed and the wooden posts were replaced by metal – although I did enjoy the time our adversary tried his chainsaw on a hingepost filled with headless, and therefore invisible, six-inch nails. Hopefully both an expensive and painful experience.

Admonition the Forty-fourth:
Every Castle Should Have a Ghost

Actually, that should read: *Every* Castle has a Ghost.

We didn't think we did.

No really, we walked into what remained of Dunans House and it didn't feel haunted. Despite the decay, the fruiting bodies, the dusting of orange spore, the wet-rot, the feeling that this was indeed the inspiration for Geiger's spaceship in the movie *Alien* – the house didn't feel active.

"Active" is Sadie's adjective. It describes a building, apartment or room which contains some non-corporeal residue of past inhabitants which is capable of interacting with present occupants at a conscious, or, more usually, subconscious, level.

An example: as a Feng Shui consultant, Sadie was often asked to visit 'problem' houses or apartments, where rooms or areas in a building were not working for the residents. In one case she was invited to a newly renovated town house in London. The interior had been completely refurbished into a mostly white, minimalist interior. However, the wife – an interior designer – could not get the house right. The new decor did not fit. It felt wrong, like a badly fitting jacket. She knew everything was objectively just as she wanted, but the place didn't feel comfortable – this feeling, and therefore the house, was putting her and her partner at odds with one another and neither of them were sleeping. Sadie says she too felt the oddness when she visited but had no idea why until she visited the master bedroom. With the couple behind her she opened the door to the bedroom and saw to her amazement, not the white clean lines she expected, and which were evident in the rest of the house, but a study fitted out in green and yellow striped wallpaper, lined with book cases, and containing a big old mahogany desk redolent with pipe tobacco smoke.

In shock, Sadie closed the door and turned to the couple in askance. They were looking at her, equally disconcerted by her unexpected reaction to what they considered their perfectly ordinary bedroom. Mystified, Sadie turned back and opened the door again.

This time, the room was as expected: a perfectly lovely minimalist interior with huge be-duveted bed. Canny to the ways of houses Sadie immediately asked the couple how the room had been decorated when they bought it twelve months before. They described the phantom room, down to the wallpaper and the stale smell of tobacco. The house was revealing an old pattern, one that the couple hadn't managed to erase with their perfect decor, and which would remain active until Sadie intervened.

In the case of Dunans, perhaps its apparent inactivity was because the space was so decayed, perhaps that no-one had really lived in the building since the 1970s or perhaps that those rooms in which activity might have occurred had no floor, or no ceiling, or even only partial walls. Certainly, what had been the laundry, and is now a bathroom, had a certain 'air' about it – one of impending doom, as did the kitchen on the other side of the stud wall. These rooms were at the back of the old house on the first floor, above the school room which ranged the full width of the gable. This meant that the six-inch-thick brick-built dividing wall between washing and cooking rooms above was virtually unsupported. Or rather, it had been built on top of six-inch wide, one-inch-thick pine tongue and groove floorboards, which in turn were fixed to a series of eight by two joists, hung, in a somewhat compromised manner, on a wall plate affixed to crumbling fifteenth-century mixed rubble walls. The damp-soaked lath and plaster on ceiling and wall, added to the load, which meant that the floor dropped a good three inches to the centre. Water spilled at either doorway would migrate – cracked Lino allowing – towards the centre of each room, in rapid fashion, pooling under the wall itself where bricks met floorboard. It was, therefore, only a matter of time before said wall fell through the ceiling of the school room bringing along with it the second-storey maids' bedroom floor and associated roof above. And that would also include nail-sick west-coast slate, sarking, and spongey oak A-frame as well as a good slice of the gable with its crow-steps and chimney-stack. The potentiality of all these assorted tonnes of differentiated materiel, added to that overwhelming sense of doom, of disaster pending, of inevitability. We propped the ceiling of course, but avoided the room until the issue was properly dealt with some couple of years later.

However, certain doom does not a ghost make, despite the psychic angst it may cause in the householder.

A ghostly presence bespeaks a certain level of incorporeal agency, a sensation of spiritual intersection with the real world, a notion that there is more out there than we can possibly comprehend.

I might talk about quantum entanglement, or string theory, or somesuch.

I might talk of spiritualism, or God, or faith.

The environment holds onto the merest glimmer of our passing, like the after-effect of a strong light on a retina – for a while there is an occlusion, a shape, a fading effect, which eventually subsides. This I feel is how, aside from our physical works, our surroundings remember, or record us – and of course, the more potent the event – the more painful or wonderful or even oft-repeated – the stronger the presence. Hence: the cup of tea presented to those waking in the blue bedroom of the Old House by the grey lady (three witnesses); the tumble of dogs panting at the foot of the Castle staircase and stepped over repeatedly (two witnesses); the Irish navvy prowling the deck of Telford's Bridge at midnight on the twenty-first December each year (... but no, we have never seen him – despite brandy, and boots with thick soles and breath pluming whitely into the starless, frigid night air – despite extra batteries, and tartan Tam, and a brazier for warmth and comfort – despite belief, a photograph and the word of Rob Roy's descendant (Maternal-line); and, of course, dear old Uncle Cyril (multiple witnesses, all of whom were well-known to the author).

If the wait for the spirit of the navvy was suitably gothic and unbelievable – inconceivable even – then the ghost of Uncle Cyril had something of the modern, of the quotidian, of the credible to it.

Banish the faerie, the fêted, the fetid and the fated from your mind, and bring the post-war years to mind, those three decades ending somewhere in the late Seventies, when the shock of the Second World War had given way to a settlement in which work, routine and life in general seemed – oil-crisis, cold-war, Vietnam, Korea, Suez notwithstanding – pretty settled. Uncle Cyril, so-called because it was he, who along with his redoubtable wife, Isa, provided a measure of *loco parentis* for two local scallywag boys, one of whom was to become Fletcher Clan Chief, and the other to reprise his genetically sealed fate of buckling-swash and dead-eye shot – albeit with caman and clay rather than claymore and slingshot. These many-storied youths spent their formative years prowling Cyril's demesne – the policies of Dunans – for which he was groundsman.

And herein we establish the necessary routine for a long shadow, or after-presence, or gentle haunting. Cyril was known for his trout tickling, his roll-up smoking, and his special brew habit. It was also entirely appreciated that once inside the house, within his wife's, the house-keeper's, domain, such habits, apart from the tickling of the trout of course, were not to be entertained. Therefore, between knocking-off at five-thirty and returning to the house at six, a pause was established, for the gutting of the fish, and the drinking of the special brew, and the smoking of the tobacco, and the reading of the news, and the sitting quietly in masculine solitude – unless the scallywag boys interrupted it, for tales, and slightly stale biscuits. Thereafter, once the allotted time had passed – a time we assume negotiated through the unspoken colloquy of clocks and pauses and tuts – the gentleman tramped to the house, passing through the gravelled kitchen garden, the nascent *rhododendron* hedges, and the last remnants of the old gaffer's barely-trimmed box.

And on entering of course there would be the scrubbing of the hands, the slight stupor of the alcohol and the chewing of the leaf of mint to mask the tobacco – albeit with the attendant knowing of the wife.

The blue overall would be hung against the door, the woollen cap over the collar curved atop the door-hook and the boots set beside the hearth. An entirely civilised mug of tea would then appear at his elbow as he sat down at the kitchen table, and he would compose himself to the day as reported by his estimable partner and helpmeet.

Here ends our direct knowledge, garnered wholly from a later conversation with our neighbour, and confirmed through Cyril himself, thusly –

After twelve, or even eighteen months in the red shed, we had extended parts of it to accommodate infants, and chattels, and fuel-making processes as already noted. My business had migrated to an external shed, and we were gradually taming the plant life around us. Part of that was the clearance of the *rhododendron ponticum* – again, as already noted. As the thickly-wrought matt of trunk, branch, leaf and purple flower was cleared, using chainsaw, handsaw, lever, rake, harsh language and intermittent bonfire, we – that is the inhabitants of the Red Shed – began to fear one of us was a secret smoker.

We discounted the copious amounts of smoke rising from the highly calorific logs the rhodie supplied, and the knuckles of (apparently) smokeless fuel we supplemented our stove with, and the bonfires which were finished mid-afternoon, and the thought that somehow this was the scent of the castle still emitting post-conflagration fumery.

No, it was clear to both myself and Sadie that the faint acrid scent, was none of these things, partially because it always happened between five-thirty and six, when we were preparing the girls for bed; partially, because it was only noticeable in the north end of the shed where the beds were – the girls' and ours; and more particularly, because that smell was of a hand-rolling tobacco, a scent we had both grown accustomed to as I completed the long journey to stop smoking the year we arrived, before Eldest was born, as also previously noted. Every evening it seemed one or both of us would notice the soft scent of second-hand smoke and look at the other askance, as if to say, "Have you …?" or "Surely not…" And after a moment, underlying that middle note, was an accompanying bass line of beer, the cloying, sugary closeness of 7%+ brown liquid.

These things we would have ignored, could have ignored, but for the figure who paced the grounds intermittently. Dressed in a blue overall, wearing a beanie and with a pronounced stoop.

Sadie and I both caught sight of him "out of the corner of our eye" as we did the washing-up, or laid the fire, or worked facing one of the back windows in the living room. We caught his shape, the impression, of a thin man walking behind the shed.

As ever we were employing folk to clear the grounds, make paths, begin renovations of the house, so it wasn't unusual to see a man walking behind the shed.

But on a Sunday? Or at eight in the morning? Our hackles were very active after a couple of months of this.

However, it was Kirsteen – a local who worked for me for a year or so – who finally convinced us both we weren't victims of over-active imagination.

One afternoon, with no-one onsite, but Sadie and herself, Kirsteen was making a cup of something in the kitchen of the red shed. She glanced up, and as myself and Sadie had done so many times, caught the shape of someone walking around the back of the shed.

"Sadie?" she said.

"Hmm?" Sadie replied, with either laptop or youngest on her lap.

"Is there anyone working here today?"

"Er… No, Charlie is off in Dunoon and Mike is back to Arran for the summer. Why?"

"Well, I've just seen someone go around the back of the shed."

There is a pause, a beat, a moment of barely concealed consternation.

"Blue overall? Beanie? Stooped?"

"Aye, that's him."

"We're not sure who it is."

"You're not sure?"

Now, if you know anything about Sadie and myself by this point in the story, you'll know that in most things, we *are* sure. Or at least forthright. We don't let things lie. Well, I might, but only until I have had a proper think about it and constructed an intricate strategy with decision-tree and a series of contingencies, most of which don't come to pass, both because they are so unlikely, and also because once I am decided I am decided and therefore the contingencies don't get a look in at all. Obstinate would be the word for me. And as for Sadie, she considers all angles in a nanosecond and can therefore be even more decided than I on an immediate basis. So, expressing uncertainty at any point in our career at Dunans would strike anyone, and, in particular, Kirsteen, who knew us well at that point, as very unusual.

"No, we aren't. We think he's the smoker in the evening."

"Oh?"

"Yes. We think the rhodie clearance this Spring woke him."

"Woke him?" It may have been at this stage that Kirsteen's entirely justified incredulity would have caused the conversation to falter, possibly even causing her to exclaim "Ye Gads, these are rum folk!", run from the shed, jump in her car and drive for the south with all due alacrity. However, fortuitously at that moment there was a knock on the doorframe, a knock which all at the Red Shed were familiar. It was our neighbourly neighbour McGuffy, calling round for a coffee and a chat.

Now the thing about McGuffy is that he is as straight as an arrow, even a Fletcher one. If anyone was to embody the clan's motto *Recta Pete*, or 'Aim for Right Things', that would be the McGruff. Not that he is anything to do with the Fletcher bloodline – partial and contended as it is – but living a short walk down the glen, he has known the folks at Dunans, in all their varieties, intimately, and therefore, now, might claim that that motto has as much relevance to him as to whoever inhabited Dunans. But then again, such circumlocution, or sentimentality would cut no ice, fleece, or tree with him, cut of the cloth of heroes as he is (of which more elsewhere). In this case, in unknowingly heroic mode, he provided an immediate and steadying explanation for the elusive personage haunting the grounds at Dunans that early summer.

On receiving the description of aforesaid apparition, and having meantime been served a large mug of cafetiere coffee, with four spoons and a dashing dash of semi-skimmed, plus offered squashed flies or cowardly creams, he opined, quite without reservation, "Aye, that'll be Uncle Cyril." And here he told of Cyril's routine, of his own scallywag youth, the tickling of trout and Isa's lemon drizzle cake – which of course was the natural companion to the very civilised cup of char.

Needless to say, thereafter, Uncle Cyril was addressed at every corner-of-the-eye appearance, every whiff of second-hand smoke, each rumour of hop or fish, with a decidedly friendly, "Evening Cyril!" or "Thank you very much Cyril!" or "It's alright Uncle Cyril we are looking after the old place …!" That latter once we'd consulted our intuition and decided that perhaps, just perhaps, the old guy was somewhat discombobulated by the state of the house and the recovery works we were now attempting in his beloved (or otherwise) garden.

Admonition the Forty-fifth:
Do Not Sit Next to a
Midge Magnet

I promise, this is the last entry I will make on midges – this is *not* an obsession, it's just a facet of life living on the West Coast that requires a proper level of attention, and I am not sure those who do not live here recognize how debilitating the early to mid-summer miniscule airborne assault is. But this admonition is really to help us understand the effect the midge has on visitors as much as on residents – at least visitors who don't read the instructions on the side of the packet labelled, "Holidays In Argyll".

The Midge Magnet is a *magnet*.

Midges, seeking the carbon dioxide exhaled by animals are attracted to it – as if it's a … magnet.

By sitting there you're creating a HUGE target for midges, even those outside the quarter acre of previously cleared midge-free environment – because a midge magnet, run for several weeks can clear a quarter of an acre pretty effectively.

If you sit around one, it'll not be pretty.

Having settled, spread out your picnic blanket, ranged your various edibles in an artful crescent of plenty and poured your drinks, you'll start to feel the odd miniscule bite. The first few, yes, you will ignore, thinking that you are sitting beside a midge magnet and the midge bites you are are receiving are outliers, are just the residual infestation which for the most part has been dealt with. But after a further five or six seconds the frequency of bites will have become intense, and as long as you are wearing your glasses, even smeared with the mayonnaise you wiped up from your youngest's attempt at filling her burger bun, you start to see that this is not an isolated pod of midge but a swarm. That realisation will lift you to your feet in a wild convulsion. You'll spill your beer, knock the prosecco for six, throw down your burgers in panic, trample small children – all the time swearing, "Bloody-bastarding-thing doesn't bastarding work. You said they worked! Only reason I agreed to come here. Right, I have had enough Mildred, WE ARE LEAVING!"

You will all then jump into your seven-year-old Volvo and never return, even to retrieve the youngest's purple unicorn pillow called Tilly from your accommodation, which a week later a family wanting respite from a midge-infested patch of grounds near a castle not twenty miles away, will find in the porch, hanging rather forlornly on a coat-hook.

Admonition the Forty-sixth: Stalkers are not easily stalked

Every year for quite a while, we benefitted from the stalking skills of various parties. There's a team of carpet fitters from Glasgow, a trio of ex-Servicemen who came to us via Sadie's second cousin and a bunch of youngsters from over the hill who make money bringing in the Antipodean relations of a local well-to-do family. venison, whisky, and coffee regularly arrived at the front door, along with one or several of these enthusiasts. During the season one or other of the groups would come in at one end or the other of the range and spend the early mornings creeping about *Maol Odhar* ("Bald Man" in Scots Gaelic), stalking the stags and does as they flitted through the stands of Sitka and larch. I never joined any of the parties, not that I was invited or ever really interested, but we saw each regularly as they brought carcasses off the hill via the bridge – it being the only way across the river below the hill for miles.

Late one morning in early October, as I was making my final cup of coffee of the day, I heard the distinctive rumble of a diesel quad picking its way down the hill. As the ATV neared, I stepped out of my office, mug in hand, to work out which of the stalkers were making their slow way across the fore paddock. They'd been successful and were balancing a huge red stag across the back of the vehicle. They saw me and waved, and then, to my surprise, one of them walked over as soon as they reached the more stable ground of the drive.

"That's quite a size!"

"I know, I know!" smiled Davey, "We were lucky with that one. Shot in a million. He spooked as Archie fired." he paused, "We're okay to use the bridge still?"

"Yeah, of course! No problems."

"That's good, that's good."

"Why do you ask?"

"Ah, well we thought you might be using the woodlands for …" his voice dropped, "… activities."

"What?" I was surprised, "No, we don't own it. We think it's changed hands recently, so we're not sure who actually owns it."

"Oh, okay. That's good." I raised my eyebrows inquisitively, "No, see, we just saw something strange." He paused, "Someone strange. It's what spooked the stag."

"Oh?"

"Yeah, and that's why I'm asking. We thought you might be doing some adventure activities or something. You know, backwoods training or some sort of war-games. Paint-balling mebbe?"

"God no! They did that when they opened the castle as a hotel. But us? No. And not the old owners of the woodland either – they were never here. Or not often at least. They were/are down south somewhere I think."

"So that's even stranger then." he paused again to think, "See, Archie was about to take the shot. All perfect. In profile, facing into the glen. Didn't know we were there – just a couple of hundred metres upwind. You know? And then as he fired – at the exact same time – there was a noise downhill. The stag startled, but just a moment too late. For the stag I mean. Round must have hit him as he spooked, but still. He kind of fell in a half-leap. Made getting at him a real bastart. Had to use a block and tackle to drag him out of that burn. Caught in the roots of a big, old Alder.

He paused, collecting himself, "So, as Archie re-loaded the Tikka, I looked down the hill, and there he was, at the tree line, staring up. Saw the whites of his eyes first. Like he was caught in headlights. Was dressed in black and a balaclava. Had a rucksack. Almost blended into the pines behind him. Soon as he saw I'd seen him, he turned back into the coup. Archie'd seen him too. He said, 'Well, you don't see that every day, not on this hill.'"

"No, I guess not!" I said.

"No, last person we'd seen up there was KP's eldest looking for his dog. But that was a long time ago." Davey shook his head, "Anyway, this was bloody odd, the bloke in the balaclava I mean. Real odd. Thing was, way this bloke was moving, he wasn't a spring chicken. And he wasn't a woodsman either. The gear maybe helped him think he was, but. No, he moved like he was in his sixties. Careful – slightly uncertain – shoulders tensed – hands out in case of a fall. What he was doing up there, early morning I have not a Scoob." He paused again, shaking his head as if wondering about the foolishness of some people, "Anyway, thought I'd ask just in case you were doing stuff up there. You know, make sure everyone stays safe while we're shooting."

"Aye thanks – no, no, you're fine. Fine. And whoever it was, was nothing to do with us. Cannot imagine what he was doing up there." I scratched my chin wondering whether to voice my suspicions. I decided not. "I'm just glad the shot was clean. Would've not been good to get a runner." A thought occurred to me, "So what time was this?"

"Sun'd just come up. Maybe just before six? We've had a couple that have not been as clean as we'd like, but Archie's two are the business. Real good trackers. Not distracted."

"Yeah, I've seen them. Nice brace." I paused to take a sip of my coffee, thinking, "So whoever it was was up there very, very early. That is bloody weird. Did you see them again?"

"Well, nooo. But there was definitely someone about the quad before I fetched it. We'd dragged the stag out of the burn and while Archie did the necessary, I hoiked off to get the bike. So, I got down maybe fifty minutes after we saw that idjit. And it was like someone had been walking around the bike and my car. You know peering in. Checking it out. Nosey fucker. Footprints all around. Looked like Hunters. You know, those ribbed grips an' rounded heels. Not big big. Maybe sevens or eights. He obviously had a good look then skipped off to the road."

"Hunters. Hmm. Either he's got a bit of cash behind him or he doesn't know what the soil round here does to boots like those. Do you think he did anything?"

"Nah, he was just nosing, walking around. Don't think he got close enough. Didn't see anything that looked like he'd got close enough to tamper. Don't like it though. Not at all."

"No, nor I, nor I."

There was a tinny blarp from the others on the ATV. "Right, I'll be off! Mebbe see you in a fortnight! Mebbe have something for youse."

"That'd be good – and if you see him again …"

"Yeah, we'll let you know Charlie! Cheers!"

Admonition the Forty-seventh: Try Your Very Best Not to Play Shinty

Shinty is very like hockey.

Except there are fewer rules.

And it is more brutal.

And they wear kilts.

No, they don't wear kilts, or at least they don't when they are playing.

Anyway, this is a game for players who really don't mind losing eyes, breaking bones or foregoing sensation in any and all limbs.

It helped that I'd never seen a game played for real before I joined Col-Glen Shinty Club. It also helped that McGuffy, who was my entry point for the team, was not loquacious about the sport in the way that Ronnie, or KP, or Bogey were. Had they been persuading me it would have been a tale of blood and guts, of lost eyeballs, dislocated knees and broken ankles. Instead, McGuffy plied his trade over several weeks and multiple cafetieres of coffee, he ate my biscuits, and chucked my hounds under their chins, and charmed Sadie, and told stories of glory, of the beginnings of the club, of days of yore, of the gold and the black taking the field and winning through skill and strategy. No brute force. No wild hits. No shoulder-barging. We were to be the proponents of *total-shinty*.

And following on from these briefings, weekly shinty

practice was great fun. Lots of laughs. But there was more physical contact than I thought entirely necessary, and the practice balls regularly reached mach-3 as they whistled towards the goal at head height.

It was all slightly unnerving.

Unlike practice, playing a competitive match is truly terrifying.

Fig. 3 – The "Ancient Warrior Game", also known as Shinty

For example, there is a rule that if you fall over, it is your fault, and you should get up immediately. If you don't get up immediately, then your team is penalised, despite the fact that your opposite number is kicking seven shades of shit out of you as the referee looks on.

Oban Celtic, I am looking at you. Inveraray I am looking at you. Kyles Athletic I am looking at you. Ronnie, I am most especially looking at you.

Having said that, you will find my name in the Camanachd lists for scoring a goal against a Loch Fyne club away. We lost 5-2, but I still scored. An Englishman with a double-barrelled surname wielding a caman and on the score-sheet.

A highlight.

Or perhaps a matter of the depths the Glen had to go to field a full team.

In the lead-up to my second season playing, I broke a rib in practice. Or rather, Lochie – long, tall, densely muscled Lochie ran into me, and his elbow broke my rib – or it could have been his little finger – or his earlobe.

We laughed.

How we laughed.

A season-and-half was enough. Was it the rib you ask? Was it the concussion? Was it the thumb that had ceased moving? Or perhaps, the screaming of the coach? The big bugger from Ardrishaig clouting me across the knee? Was it the beer-fuelled journeys back from matches along precipitous, winding, slippery roads with overfilled bladders? The line of players pissing against the prevailing wind? The urine splattered knees and shoes and hands?

None of these.

No.

And all of them.

If you ask me why I played, I am still not sure, but once a promise is made – even under the influence of a bottle and half of the hooch they call a single malt – because that is, after all, what it took – it is made.

Admonition the Forty-eighth: Professionals Require Careful Consideration

Inevitably you will need an architect. Maybe even a team of architects. A Firm. And also, a QS and a Structural Engineer. You'll need these to fulfill the requirement of local council and heritage bodies to dot and cross the relevant letters. And those dots and crosses will also be important for things like mortgage companies, and insurance companies, and environmental protection agencies, and grant-giving bodies. The world requires paperwork as provenance for what is in front of you.

You'll also need these buildings professionals to help define your ideas such that they – the plans you have – become acceptable to the aforementioned external stakeholders. Also, oftentimes, these professionals will help you dismiss your ideas in favour of their ideas, which while impracticable or indefensibly expensive, are the latest design concept they wish to express through their client's wallet – your wallet.

With these ideas in mind, we spent quite a time looking at Architects. Quite a time. It took several meetings to find someone who we were comfortable with. And comfortable is a relative term.

After all this time, the meetings with the different candidates agglomerate into a template which we grew quite accustomed to.

At the appointed time, or a little before, two cars would appear. Expensive cars. Often cars which were rugged but smart. The kind of smart which had panels of stainless steel or carbon in inappropriate areas of bodywork highlighting an aggressive grill or a butch wheel arch. Gentlemen, and it was mostly gentlemen, would slide out of these under-utilised behemoths in sleek slacks and shiny shoes, tip-toe around dogs and toys, rashes and stobs to shake my hand and then Sadie's, sniff the air and then retreat to get jacket or gilet, because it was a "few degrees cooler than town." Ties would be surreptitiously loosened or discarded, and wellies would be shaken out ready for site inspection while comments would be made about the drive and being glad, they'd brought out the "Tonka toy". We'd have half-an-hour walking around house and castle. Sadie and I would talk in general terms about what we were considering, and then, with the senior architects (as there were often two) we'd go and have a coffee and a discussion. The junior team would be left to take photos and measurements. And once the niceties of coffee production and serving were negotiated, often with exclamations of surprise at the very serviceable latté or cappuccino served from the galley in our "very neat" or "surprisingly spacious" or "carefully considered" living space, we'd hear about their offer. And the costings guidelines. And how they'd design and run the job.

At this point, or sometimes before, a glossy brochure would slide over the table, with leaflets on technology or contractors or further consultants. There'd be a case study or two. All of it on heavy-weight paper, with heavy-weight branding and reassuringly expensive looking offices displayed on the back alongside their contact details. I'd weigh these in my hand, and Sadie would glance over at me with an arched eyebrow.

We would then ask the two questions, the ones that really mattered: how much did they think it would cost, and secondly, how much were they going to charge? If you know this industry, you will know in broad terms, architects charge as a percentage of the final cost of the works. In every case, except one, the fee would be six-figures. In every case, except one, the project would graze eight figures, and in every case, but one, there was no space to recognise the reality that the building would demand of us: that when finished there needed to be a business case to support the project, to support the prodigious cost.

No, that was entirely our bailiwick apparently.

Perhaps I am being unfair to those that journeyed out to us, over the Rest or on the ferry – they mostly chose the boat, I think. Perhaps the business case for the whole thing was a brass tack we'd get to after the heads of terms were agreed – or something like that – but, to me, to Sadie, this idea of putting a finger to the wind to determine the cost of a project which was so idiosyncratic and so beset with (in some cases) unrecognised or (in other cases) obvious constraints, without examining in detail the business case we would eventually put the building to, seemed ridiculous. If we were to invest seven figures, or even eight, we'd need a partner who would have the end point, the earning potential, the customers, the business case at the forefront of their mind.

Or at the least would understand that this was a primary design constraint.

I am. I am being unfair. And perhaps also reflecting the naivety with which we approached this aspect of the project at the time.

We used a different strategy some seven or eight years later when we recruited Robin Kent, who was, by all measures, the most successful of our professional interlocutors in the physical environment of the restoration – we turned his *Conservation Plan for Dunans* into a beautiful book (available from Amazon and ScottishLaird.co.uk) and continue to follow his outline for the project even now. For him, for our future author, we outlined a phased process which would have several stop points – places where we could pause indefinitely as we recharged the finances and capacity before proceeding. A piece-meal process if you like. The idea for this approach began with Martin the Method, the architect we eventually selected for the restoration of the house.

Martin arrived one overcast afternoon in a small grey hatchback. A nice hatchback, but grey and small nevertheless. We warmed to Martin. He wore walking togs, and boots, and had a careful manner, which while never being exactly enthusiastic was nevertheless persuasive of a commitment to doing the proper thing for historic buildings. He still drafted his plans in pen and ink, was a one-man operation and lived in the county. Unlike the others, the shiny brigade, he was aware of the Argyll process, the personalities, the idiosyncrasies, and even had an inkling of matters previous to our ownership, having paid attention to the fire at Dunans at the time. He'd heard the rumours, and was pleased to get some sort of coherent, and sustainable, vision from us. And while he also abided by the usual RIBA fee structures, we were able to agree to the sort of staged process – the method of the nickname – we would use as a template going forward for all our professional interactions.

Within a few months of meeting that first time, we had consents for our plans for the house from both the council and Historic Scotland, as it was termed then.

Admonition the Forty-ninth: A Note on Badgers' Hats

Invariably, the type of castles that this book can be applied to, are those sited in the middle of nowhere. This means that, while there may be badger setts locally, with the occasional sight of black and white pelts pelting away through *rhododendron* groves or silver birch stands, the phrase "It's as black as a badger's hat!" may be used truthfully and as often as you are caught in the grounds – for as we know there are grounds – without torch or phone or walkie-talkie-with-useful-light-even-when-turned-off.

And why, you may ask, are badgers' hats black? They'd not be white, would they? And then even more appositely, since when did badgers wear hats?

Admonition the Fiftieth: There Are Times to Embrace Gossip

Apparently, in nineteenth-century America, they used to call siblings with less than twelve months between them Irish twins. In Glendaruel, the phenomena is evidently attributed more to forgetfulness than heritage: Sadie was asked on three separate occasions whether I'd allowed our satellite TV contract to lapse.

Leaving aside the assumptions about who was the bill payer in our household, the primacy of our Sky subscription to our evenings' entertainment and the notion that we could not have possibly intended such a rapid 'production schedule', we were both appalled that the gossip-making-class in the Glen had not come up with more than one joke to rib us with in all their discussions about our growing family.

It was not even possible for the event of Youngest's birth to be a private matter, even if we had wanted it to be. In many ways with Eldest being born just before Hogmanay, and in Glasgow, we'd not experienced the full weight of the chatter and anticipation that a new infant provokes in a small community, one which really doesn't have much to talk about. Or maybe, that first year, we just weren't particularly attuned to the local chat. With Youngest's arrival, all the circumstances seemed to ensure everyone knew everything immediately. For one thing, Youngest was born, locally, in Dunoon at the Community Hospital. For another, she rather caught us by surprise, and because she did, I was unable to convey Sadie modestly and steadily to the midwifery unit.

We were at home waiting. I knew Sadie was having mild contractions, but she was managing them using a Tens machine and I was working in the grounds. I poked my head in the door and asked her how she was doing. "Four" she said.

"Four?"

"On the dial. On the Tens machine. Out of ten." she answered shortly. I saw she was painting a wall and listening to Pratchett's *Going Postal.*

"Riiight. Okay I'll come back in half an hour."

Ten minutes later as I was stripping out brambles from the Ha-ha, I heard a noise above me. I looked up. Sadie was there, swaying, pale, mouthing my name. I leapt up, "Darling?"

"I'm at five!" She said.

"Okay?"

"Out of five." She rolled her eyes, "Midwife, rang. Told me the dial only had five." Another contraction started. "We need to go. Now!"

Ninety seconds later Sadie was strapped into the passenger seat of Boris with her grab-bag and droplets of fuchsia paint in her hair, Eldest was in the new toddler car seat, and all three of the dogs were in the boot.

We roared down to the Caravan Park and dropped Eldest into Godmother No. 1's out-stretched arms. As Sadie contracted another time, I turned the car crunching the gears and swearing. I could see our Newf in the rear-view mirror had settled his jollops on the top of the backseat between the head rests, his soulful eyes flicking between me frantically squeezing the last joule of energy out of our lumbering Disco, and Sadie equally frantically trying to hold back the inevitable.

We had a thirty-minute car ride along a single-track road. It was a Thursday. It was lunchtime. If we were lucky, we'd already missed folks returning from their morning at the shops. If not, oncoming traffic could delay us considerably. Looking across at Sadie who was gripping the grab bar on the dash as hard as she could, we couldn't afford any delays.

When we turned off the A-road onto the single-track that took us across the hills of Cowal to Dunoon, there was a car at the 'T' junction. As I jammed our elderly disco into second and thumped down on the accelerator, I got a blurred impression of one of the older ladies of the glen looking up at our careening green four-by-four and knew in that instant that even before we arrived at the midwifery unit, the whole community would know Sadie had gone into labour. It made the subsequent head-on vehicular encounters with hotelier, councillor, forester, convener of the Women's Institute and the postman easier to bear – I felt no compunction flashing lights, honking the horn, and using indicators to make our hurry obvious and undeniable. Afterall, because of that first encounter, I knew that Youngest's arrival was already likely to be passing from receiver-to-receiver on the well-established phone network of the glen. The flurry of passing places, curious bystanders and the single, gesticulating, bad-mouthing driver were neither here nor there for my calm, focussed and deeply breathing wife.

Sadie was utterly centred.

Well, mostly.

She did swear a bit.

We swerved around the end of the hospital and drove up to the main doors. I parked on the yellow grid of 'thou-shalt-not-park-here' lines, threw open the door and rushed around the side of the car to find three midwives already handing Sadie out of the car. There were no questions, not many words either – all of them were focussed on getting my wife into the unit. They could see the baby was imminent.

As I stood, slightly at a loss, I heard Sadie growl, "Pool!"

Two hours later, I arrived back in the glen, with the dogs, to pick up Harry, and everyone – *everyone* – knew. Weight, sex, time of birth and even, it seemed, the temperature of the water in the birthing pool.

That evening Sadie wet Youngest's head in hospital with Godfather No. 1 who had managed to sneak in a bottle of Courvoisier past the midwives.

I managed to avoid more than a single finger of malt at Eldest's Godmother's but was nabbed by Hamilton on the West Road and therefore had to share a nip of Rusty Nail from his hip flask – that certainly explained his erratic droving habits. He waved at Eldest through the car window as we discussed the reproductive proclivities of the folks in the Glen, "that lot down on the Kyles" and his sheep. We mostly talked about his sheep, and the lambing season he'd had. "Terrible," he said, "terrible. But then," he went on, in an odd segue, "every family hereabouts has a third. It's the rule. So, you'll be having a third, eh? Soon as you can, I expect." There was definitely an evil twinkle in his eye. I have to say I did look at him askance. As if in defence he maintained that that was what all the talk in the Glen was about. And after all, the school roll had a gap coming up, and a third from us would cover it handily. Couldn't let those buggers at Lochgilphead close our school. No, a third from us would be just the ticket, especially as we were in our prime. He nudged me, "You're in your prime, aren't you? Eh Charlie?" waggled his eyebrows and laughed uproariously. I think – *I think* – the question and thereby the implication were ironic, if not a direct comment on the Glen and its chatterers.

As we drove away along the long straight to Achenelid I chuckled ruefully, thinking, well, at least that's one who understands how gossip can be both intrusive and silly at the same time. And informative - it was evident that Hamilton had heard mutterings about schools at the Market, or the Lodge or the Kirk, and in Argyll, that meant something serious was afoot. Indeed, some years later when both Eldest and Youngest were at the school in question just such a plan was announced – it drew our little community together, and the proposed closure was roundly defeated.

At the junction between the old road and the main road I met KP who waved at me to pause. We often stopped and chatted. Often about nothing in particular, mostly shinty, but at times it had proven useful to keep him updated on our doings. After the obligatory congratulations and questions after mother and child, and a wave at Eldest who was starting to become restive, KP's tone took on a more serious tenor, "Charlie, I wanted to let you know that the batman has been seen about prowling in the early mornings over the last couple of months."

"Batman? Oh, do you mean …Well, I want to say Haggis, or Hamish, or …?

"Yes, you've got the man – the one Old Donald caught by the ankle that time and tipped into the half-emptied slurry pit."

"Ugh, that would have been rank."

"Not the word. But. Look. Me and the missus think he's been prowling up by us, and I wouldn't be surprised …"

"If he comes across the river."

"Aye."

It was then I remembered Davey's account of someone on the hill that day.

KP's eyes glinted, "That sounds right. Just be careful. He's not. Careful I mean, and he's out there looking for dirt."

"Dirt?"

"Oh, anything and everything. You see him one night

and a week later there's been an anonymous complaint to the RSPCA, or SEPA …"

"Or the council."

"Ah, yes, the hoteliers. That would've been right."

"Alright, thanks KP. Forewarned is forearmed."

"He plays dirty Charlie. I know you'll not be afraid to go to the law, but he's canny that one. Canny and vicious."

Sadie and Youngest returned home a day later, and once Eldest and Youngest had been put to bed with nursery rhymes and lullabies respectively, Sadie and I discussed this latter exchange as we wet the baby's head with a celebratory bottle of fizz and piquant curry. We recognized that given KP's posture towards us – as friendly and encouraging – his warnings were worth listening to, but also, that, again, this was gossip. The pejorative term "Batman", and the rumours that swirled about his conduct could be nothing to us, nor guide our behaviour until we encountered it directly.

In fairness, we had to treat as we found rather than as we heard – we would not prejudge.

Admonition the Fifty-first: A Cup of Tea is Essential to Keep the Team Happy

If you have self-built or self-restored or even commissioned any significant building work here in the UK, you will know the importance of builders' tea or 'BT': not only that everyone on site drinks at least a dozen cups a day, but that you have to make a good mug to ensure workforce morale.

It helps too if you smoke.

Or did.

Or at least can provide matches.

Smoking or possibly vaping (though I have no experience of the latter) has been an integral part of the tea taste experience for years and shouldn't be discounted lightly in the building site experience of tea drinking. The cloying sweetness of a good BT can be cut through by a drag of Golden Virginia or similar. Prefabs are, in my view, too polluted with additives – like *saltpetre* – oh – and filter. This is not to say a fag is necessary, or even desirable, it's just that for historical purposes, one needs to see that a cigarette until recently has been a virtually compulsory condiment.

A big Newfoundland is helpful too – not as a condiment obviously, but to finish discarded mugs left on the floor, ensuring that next tea-break is presented with a "sparkling" set of crockery.

The builders' tea which would achieve the equivalent of three Michelin stars for the maker takes practice and an ability to distinguish in microseconds between multiple tea shaded pantones as well as the respective mash- and sledge- hammers of sweetness.

Critical BT elements are:

1.   a big mug. Preferably with a sweary joke on the outside, or for a fuller flavour, inside on the bottom as well. It needs to be a big receptacle for the purposes of ensuring adequate hydration in the squad member, but also to retain tea-heat to the bottom of the vessel – this is especially important for the self-styled raconteur of the group, who will, it is true, spend more time gassing than drinking, smoking, laughing or farting, but will still insist on a properly hot cup of char to the end of the mug and / or break.

2.   boiling water. Not for the purposes of flavour as refined tea-baggers would have it, but so the tea remains hot for as long as possible, particularly after the violent pressing – (3) below – and multiple silver spoons – (4) below.

3.   Violent pressing (VP). For a deep mahogany colour, despite full-fat milk and below-mentioned epic quantities of refined Tate & Lyle. VP is achieved with plenty of greased elbow and an over-large teaspoon (otherwise the already heroic number of four teaspoons of sugar becomes a teeth-crackingly legendary seven). The deep colour of a good builders' tea will visually presage the hot, sweet assault when you drink it.

4.   1 bag of Tate & Lyle Silver Spoon a day. To sweeten and render the correct stiff tea-texture, in which teaspoon stands momentarily. The legend of the permanently upright utensil is an overstatement. What you need to see as you lift your hand from the spoon is a momentary hesitation, and then a smooth fall in an arc centred on the tip of the spoon sitting on the bottom of

the mug. If either the spoon tip slips to the side of the mug or, the fall is as sudden as you'd expect in water or, if the jangle of the spoon hitting the side of the mug speaks to a jostling, and a multiple impact, and therefore a lack of meniscal tension in the liquid – well, then, I am afraid you will have failed to provide a cup of the requisite viscosity.

Now you might ask, what of the *actual* ingredients?

Well, bags are essential. You will not have time to muck about with loose tea, no matter how flavourful and subtle. As you will have gathered, subtlety will be entirely wasted. The jury is still out on round, square or triangles, and I think, is influenced by the fact that various brands have different technologies. For me it's about the blend …

And a good blend is essential. Yorkshire. Scottish. Cheap is ideal of course because the more dusting included with leaves the thicker the texture.

Milk is important. Just on the turn can invoke disgust or, depending on the audience, reminiscence about growing up. Full fat is better – again thicker. Skimmed works, but its thinness mitigates against the overall effect. No, the lactal fizz behind your back teeth of a full fat or even, gold top, as lactose and sucrose interact is an essential part of the experience – although the richness of the gold top might just be *too* luxurious.

Biscuits are the compulsory condiment. We began with variety boxes, road-tested all-comers then settled on Rich Tea, Gingernuts and Bourbons. The deciding factor was the performance of each having been dipped.

All other things being equal, you are now ready to recruit your team and begin the restoration – in our case, of the house, rather than the castle.

Admonition the Fifty-second: Selecting Your Tradesmen is a Critical Step

While we waited to receive planning and listed building consent through the good offices of Martin the Method, we began to assemble a team of independent builders. This is where Sadie's remarkable networking skills proved invaluable: within short order, to add to Magic Mike's plumbing and carpentry, Sadie had found Malcolm, with experience of joinery, and Ken, who trained as a structural engineer – both of whom were keen to finish off their storied careers with a memorable restoration project. These would make the core of our team – our three musketeers – and would be supported ably by Russell, an Australian, whose profession as an anaesthetist was not strictly relevant to the work in hand, but whose migrant status required that he wait several months for either re-certification or re-qualification in the UK – I don't remember which. While he waited, he laboured for the three and a bond was formed, such that by the end of the project had become a veritable d'Artagnan to the trio.

Now obviously, it was not possible for three guys to encompass all the skills necessary for a house such as Dunans, so elements were contracted out. Our sparks was both quick and thoughtful, though I was never sure whether he was called Alisdair or Alaistair, or Allaster, or Alyster, or Allystair, or Allistier – I was only sure if I had his invoice in front of me – and even then, his business partner sometimes seemed to be confused.

And slating was – inevitably it seemed at the time – provided by Robbie the Slater. Like Wee Willie the Sweep, Robbie was a well-kent figure in Dunoon and nothing if not eccentric – a body builder with a preternatural ability to shape, pierce, place and fix west coast slate to the six-by-one sarking boards lining our new roof, he spent all his time at Dunans whistling through his complete set of dentures and sucking on Werther's original butter candies. We still, occasionally, find the golden wrappers from Robbie's time at Dunans lodged in gutters and grates around the place. Until I became used to it my heart would quicken whenever I saw one glinting in the mud, thinking finally we had struck gold!

Alongside this core cast, we employed several folks on-site whose names and distinctions fade into obscurity but who arrived daily from Dunoon, sometimes for a day, sometimes for a week or three. The pace and demands of the work however meant that these short-term labourers are now only recorded in my mind as a name, or a face, but rarely, categorically as both.

Admonition the Fifty-third:
The Building Will School You
(& Everyone Else for that Matter)

Before the Castle was added in 1864, Dunans House was a two-and-a-half-storey double-fronted dwelling facing southward, with its front door in a central position and staircase lifting from hallway. The position of the staircase and therefore hall, was only indicated by the remains of stepped harling we found in the front face of the old house when the interstitial area between house and castle was stripped out. Mike, Sadie, and I stood in the unroofed two-storey space contemplating the remains of the pre-Victorian stair stringer and its implications for the internal layout of the old house for quite a while – it certainly explained why interstitial didn't seem to be properly tied into the front face of the house. And also, indicated how the original approach to Dunans would have delivered visitors to the house via the 'Swing Bridge', the (now-incomplete) avenue of Lime trees, and the yet-to-be renovated Lairds' Retreat – because now we saw the remnants of the original design, the castle was sited on the forecourt of the original house. Horses and the occasional carriage would have then been led away up to the stables to the rear of the Laird's establishment. The chain of logic, between shadow of stringer on wall of the house and the stabling of visitors' horses is one of many such engaging facets of restoring an old building – and while we'd experienced much the same when dealing with our maisonette off the Goldhawk Road in Shepherds Bush, Dunans House provided weekly, if not daily, examples of the same.

Fig. 4 –South Elevation of Dunans House, circa 1845, in a configuration suggested by Interstitial Stair-stringer Remnant.

But this is to get rather ahead of ourselves, because as is ever the case with old buildings, the process of renovation was neither straightforward nor as expected. To begin with there was the matter of the house schooling us. As with the remnants of stairways or doorways, so we found sometimes to our consternation, the house prevented us from fulfilling the brief as designed by Martin the Method.

One such schooling occurred when first Ken and Malcolm came to view the house. We were standing to the rear side of Dunans, squinting against a setting sun and the effects of a couple of stubbies.

It was a windy day.

Well, it had seemed to be a windy year that year, and we were used to the two cedars standing at the north end of the house sweeping back and forth like massive green paintbrushes as their canopies were buffetted in the breeze.

"Hold hard. That chimbley don't look right."

"The chimbley Malc?" Sadie asked.

"Leaning." he said, "Ken, what do you think?"

Ken moved to the left around the group to stand with Malcolm, and narrowed his eyes, "Yes, it's definitely starting to come away from the back wall. Leaning rearwards and outwards towards the cedar and us. Hmm."

"Hmm?" I asked, "What does "Hmm" mean Ken? Sounds awfully like the noise builders make when they realise there's an element of the job which is going to be expensive."

"When's the scaffolder coming?"

"Well, depends on the consent. And we're expecting that any day."

"Any day?" Ken glanced at Malcolm and then me, "If I were you, I shouldn't wait – get him in and get that scaffolded so you can take it down and have a chance of rebuilding it." He paused and then bent to his left, peering hard at the stack, "In the meantime, I'd be careful walking under that."

"Oh?"

Malcolm had moved to stand beside Ken, they were now peering at the chimney, around the other side of the cedar, "Oh, right!"

We looked at them both, and Sadie losing patience said, "Come on! What is it?"

"Well, if Ken's not mistaken…"

"And I rarely am."

"Rarely is. That there chimbley is actually moving."

"It is Malc. Moving. Side-to-side."

The two men, moved back to stand with us, putting the cedar between them and the tottering chimney.

"See, I don't think it was ever properly tied-in. You can kind of see from here, where the tree's branches almost touch the wall. Looks as though they added it when they added Grant's Cottage. Just built it up the exterior wall."

"Punched through the exterior wall with a couple of fireplaces."

"Bob's yer uncle …"

"Well, not quite Malc – they supported it with the outhouse."

"The lean-to?"

"Aye, they used the roof joists and half gable to support the stack."

"So, when the lean-to roof fell in …"

"It lost the external support and became vulnerable?"

"Exactly."

Silence. Each of us watching as the exposed square stack of stone shivered in the gusts.

"Well, what do we do?" asked Sadie.

"Don't walk under it." Ken repeated.

"Tape it off. Make sure no-one gets caught under it when it does fall."

"And hope it falls at a right angle to the house, towards the back lawn, on the other side of the tree."

"Yes," said Ken, "otherwise it falls towards us, along the backwall, and across the lean-to and those oil tanks."

"That'd crush it all."

"Damage the roof of the house too."

"How long do we have, do you think?"

"Not sure. *Can't* be sure. What do you think Ken?"

"Really, couldn't say, but not long."

After another hour of discussion about the job, including ideas regarding the scaffolding and drainage, we walked back to Malcom's van preparing for them to take their leave.

"So, we'll see you next week for preparatory work prior to permissions, at the rates discussed?"

"That's great Charlie," Ken shook my hand.

As I turned to shake Malcolm's mighty paw there was a loud crack, and I looked at him quizzically thinking he'd popped his shoulder or something.

Then as I realized a shoulder popping didn't make such a loud noise there was a series of muffled thumps.

As one we turned to face the tottering chimney to find it was no longer there.

Instead, there was a cloud of dust rising from behind the house.

The chimney had fallen at a right-angle, in the direction it was blown, across our view, behind the big cedar, onto the back lawn, like a stack of wooden blocks at the end of a game of Jenga. Remarkably, it only properly broke apart on impact, speaking to the resilience of the lime cement used when it was built over a century before.

After suitable exclamations of surprise and awe, we turned over some of the fallen rubble. All of it was shaped sandstone, and all of it had been eaten hollow by the combination of rain and Sulphur from coal soot. Much of it had broken up on impact on the uneven ground.

"Well," said Malcolm, "that answers that question." He looked at me sideways, "Least we'll not have to take it down ourselves, eh?"

Admonition the Fifty-fourth:
Get to Know the Environs
of Your Ruin

During winter nights seem endless, and days all too brief – only half-lit by a sun which scuds over the hilltops, barely touching the rime of frost formed on ruinous wall by its absence. Stoves, candle-light and hot toddies can only supply so much cheer in the long watch between Hogmanay and the Spring equinox. In that time the spirits are naturally lowered, and often accompanied by 'flu or colds – if you are a man, these are the same thing, obviously. It was as I was succumbing to one such bout of illness – a *partial* 'flu if you will – that I encountered what I initially thought was some sort of supernatural being.

In the first couple of years at Dunans, particularly during the colder months, I'd often take the dogs out walking up into the hills above the castle. We'd range about the woodlands in which our home is embosomed, getting to know the Sitka plantations and the small native copses, jumping over burns and startling, and being startled by sheep, and red deer. On one famous occasion the dogs passed within ten metres of the old fox standing on a bluff above them. Mr. Fox seemed to watch his domesticated cousins with great interest, head cocked, tail lowered and straight out behind him. I'd paused to pull a sock up, and as I placed my foot back down from the fallen larch on which it rested, I alerted him to my presence. He slipped away in the blink of an eye. The Newfoundland and Bassets were none-the-wiser.

I'd taken the dogs along the contour from the Red Shed northwards, past and through the two nearest Sitka plantations by way of the Old Sawmill. By the time we'd been walking for five minutes I was sweating heavily, and despite the persistent afternoon rain I'd undone the front of my waxed coat. I wasn't feeling great and probably should've gone back to bed nursing what I was starting to think was a bout of *actual* 'flu, but if you have ever walked with Basset hounds you will be very familiar with their long-range trot, one which they can maintain for hours. This enthusiasm I saw and despite my misgivings I decided that I would do the full round, which is to say our basic domestic forty-five-minute walk constituting a circuit following either the Telford Road or the ninety-metre contour out, fording the Alt A' Chaol Ghleann at the seventy-metre contour line and returning on the other. By the time we'd forded the river, waded through the rashes and mud up to the old road, and then threaded our way through the leggy alder and birch which lined and interrupted Telford's roadway it was getting towards dusk – or four p. m. – and I was seriously flagging. And of course, to call it dusk is to give the impression that there was a great deal of difference between daylight and night falling when it's raining stair-rods.

Even so, as we approached the point at which the track issued onto the main road, I became aware that the dogs had seen movement, or scented something. Knowing that this could presage full-throated chase-mode, especially with the hounds, I used Sadie's famous stop command, "DOWN". I capitalise it here, to indicate both the volume required, but also the intent. The word is uttered with a falling intonation such that when said properly the voice sounds as if it is swooping from a mid-tone to bass. The mouth moves from smile to pout, and there is a resonance in the chest on reaching the 'n'. In this case all three dogs listened and flattened to the ground. Nelly Basset because she was thoroughly inculcated as a puppy, Nancy Basset because the last time she hadn't – the day before – she had found herself banished to the porch for a night and Huddy because he really loved Nancy and would do everything in his power to mirror her behaviour – even if it meant he had to spend the night in the porch with her – which he often did.

I shook out the leads and attached each to the harnesses the three recumbent canines wore. Now no-one would be surprised to understand that Huddy as a Newf could pull – like a small pony – but so could the hounds. In fact, pound-for-pound Bassets are probably more powerful than Newfs – they are formidable, low-slung tractors. So, with my hearty, heavy trio fully leashed, Huddy to left, Bassets to right, we walked on, my senses straining to see or hear the source of the dogs' excitement.

And for context, I must also add that I was not wearing walking boots, nor even well-founded rubber wellington boots, but ten-pound-sterling ill-fitting wellies, with shallow sole crenellations and thin uppers. The walking boots gave me blisters – even after three years of wearing-in – and the Hunter's seams had all started leaking within three months of working in the acidic Argyllach mud. The cheapos, while uncomfortable to walk in, as well as cold, remained waterproof after three years of punishment. I say this because as I walked the last thirty or forty metres to the road, I knew that if – and when – the dogs all pulled together I would need to wedge my feet very firmly against branch, under ledge or in deep, deep mud to resist being pulled over and inadvertently releasing them. The proximity to the main road being my main concern.

Now, as fate would have it, I was watching my footing when the dogs sighted the figure. It was half-hidden behind a *rhododendron* bush some twenty metres ahead. I felt the simultaneous pull on my arms and looked up as the dogs gave voice. And by giving voice I mean the startlingly *basso profundo* of all three major-league rib cages venting deep and terrible howls of excitement or fear, at what I saw was a shadowy biped rising from all fours behind a thick bank of *rhododendron* foliage. Excitement overtook my three charges and as one they charged.

It was not that I missed my footing, more that while my feet were well-tensioned against my wide-pawed trio's pull, as previously advertised, my cheapo-wellies had no real traction on the greasy mud, leaf-litter and grass that made up the surface of the track. Therefore, I began to slide.

So here another piece of contextual information is important to impart: I ski, and have done since a child, and a major part of skiing, particularly in the mid-eighties, was staying on T-bar and Poma lifts – which means that given a pulling force and a comparatively slippery surface I immediately, subconsciously adopted the position I learned as a kid being towed up-slope.

It served me well, for five seconds or so.

Powerless to prevent them, I followed the dogs as they careered as one after the crouching, but swiftly moving creature. In the half-light, through the rain, during those fractured, juddering moments I was able to gain an impression of a shambling, awkward silhouette, passing between trunk, trail and tussock with a speed and agility belied by its higgledy-piggledy gait.

At the point our quarry slipped past the roadward gatepost of the track, and up towards the modern carriageway, our pursuit faltered. Luckily, the three leads all had loops through which I'd inserted my hands. Unluckily my forehead collided very forcefully with a low hanging branch of a less than upright beech whose plate had begun its inexorable slide downslope toward the river while the rest of the tree tried to maintain its connection with the sky by leaning away from gravity.

Beech, it should be noted, has many admirable features:

it burns well with a nice yellow flame, makes great kitchen furniture and is a magnificent addition to any woodland or park. We have two beech mantles made by a dear friend – and beautiful they are too with their blonde colour and minute, uniform grain.

But, the problem with a beech, and particularly a low-hanging branch or trunk, is that it is very, very hard. Also, as a tree, there is very little give in its habit. Also, the bark is often quite solid. And fine-grained, with long indentations. Sometimes with large prominent boluses, which given the dead wood at their centre, are even harder – if that's possible.

That is what my forehead hit.

A bolus.

Mid-brow.

And I suppose luckily, my feet were preceding me, giving me an angle to branch which allowed that blow to be more glancing than if, say, I had run into it full pelt.

I blacked out for a second.

It was evidently an eventful second. One which gave me cause to come round very quickly.

Rather than falling on my back as you might have immediately imagined, my feet apparently had wedged themselves against a hidden fallen tree trunk, and with the dogs pulling me forward, my crumpling, unsteady unconscious form was catapulted headfirst. The leads would have slackened, as for an instant I was moving faster than my canine charges. My landing, in a large area of waterlogged rash and leaf litter, brought me round. Cold mud crowded my mouth, water funnelled into my nose and rash stalks jabbed my forehead, cheekbones, and chin.

Before groaning, before lifting my head, before even taking a breath, I took inventory. My fingers worked. My toes too. I could feel mud soaking into me the whole length of my body. Reassured, I lifted myself onto hands and knees. There around me were three sets of noses, all sniffing, one whined. The largest nose moved forward. A very large pink tongue, with black spot, was extended. I received Huddy's benison. I lifted my hand to his nose and pushed him back, "Gerroff!" I gurgled. He barked, glad to see I wasn't mortally wounded.

Once I'd risen from my soggy bed of mud, rash and deciduate, ascertained that my trio of waggers were not injured by my sudden cantilever, and emptied my left boot of brackish freezing water, I decided to see if the mysterious figure I'd seen, and the dogs had scented, had left any spoor – any trepidation assuaged by the thought that while I was down there had been ample time for the figure to loop back and attempt bloody mayhem.

Our stalker was nowhere to be seen.

On the far side of the shrub the figure had emerged from there were marks – none definitive given the dry underside of the bush, but there was an indentation – say six foot long – where someone or something could have lain. As I studied this makeshift bed in the dying light, Nelly yelped to my left. The other two, alerted, pulled me over toward her.

Fifteen metres down the slope, towards the river, among a dense upthrust of birch there was a carcass. An ewe. Scraggy. But disembowelled by a half-felled tree, as if the poor animal had been flung against the trunk, broken it and then, as the top fell away, slid into the upward jut of the stump.

I shook my head, feeling faint. A car sped past above us painting the bloody scene with a sidewash from its full beam headlights. No, I could see the break in the tree was not related to the death – it was just an illusion wrought by the half-light. But however, it had died, the corpse was still steaming, and the trunk was slick with blood. As I stared my mouth dried, was this a kill? Had I disturbed some blood thirsty denizen of the hills as it hunted? Was violent nature, red in tooth and claw, visiting our end of the glen. And as I stood there dumbfounded and nauseous the scavenging instincts of my trio suddenly came online. As one they pulled.

"DOWN!" I cried, annoyed with myself for standing there like an idiot and allowing the dogs time to take in this gruesome scene with all its foul coppery scent. I'd have to give KP a ring when I got back home because there was no doubt given the placement and colour of the dab of spray-paint on its shoulder that this was his animal. And also, I'd no doubt he'd know exactly how the ewe had met her end in that tree. I was not going to engage in useless and frightening speculation. That could wait until I'd had word from a farmer who'd seen it all and my fever had subsided.

I dragged the dogs away and up towards the junction of track and road. By now it was too dark to track anything, let alone some predating, shambling thing.

Whatever I'd seen that afternoon was beyond my fevered, head-wrung wit.

We slogged home perplexed, exhausted, and not a little bruised.

Only later, after a steamy bath and a sinus-clearing hot toddy, did I think of Davey, of that early-morning tree-line sighting and then of KP's reports of a shadowy figure prowling the glen. And then, as I ruminated, I began to wonder whether the periodic ruination of our drivehead was connected. I wondered whether all this could be KP's "Batman", or whether was it some other actor? Was it a Haslet or a Haggis, or were they acting in concert?

Could it be that we were dealing with a constellation of interests, aligned in one purpose, but from different angles, and with different, or even, competing interests?

I could not say now whether I was in an entirely rational frame of mind at that point. I think I might have been more shaken by the vision of the dead ewe hanging in the tree than I'd've liked to admit.

In any event, it seems to me now that this was the point at which our *Offal Brethren* started to properly delineate themselves.

About the Author

Charles Dixon-Spain lives with his wife, Sadie, and two teenage offspring in a house attached to a castle reached by a bridge in a glen on a peninsula in Scotland. Charles began the ScottishLaird project in 2007 and works on it full-time to this day. With a Masters in New Literatures in English from Hull University, two decades in publishing, both online and in print, as well significant time spent in Community Development as volunteer and consultant, Charles adheres to the Fourth Admonition in this first part of How to Restore a Castle: "Always take the next step."